# FAITH
## OUTSIDE THE WALLS

Why People Don't Come and
Why the Church Must Listen

*Dedicated to my loving wife, Pam,*
*who brings joy and love into my life*

# FAITH OUTSIDE THE WALLS
### *Why People Don't Come and*
### *Why the Church Must Listen*

Ron D. Dempsey

SMYTH & HELWYS
PUBLISHING, INC.
MACON, GEORGIA

ISBN 1-57312-096-0

*Faith Outside the Walls*
*Why People Don't Come and Why the Church Must Listen*

Ron D. Dempsey

Copyright © 1997
Smyth & Helwys Publishing, Inc.

6316 Peake Road
Macon, Georgia 31210-3960
1-800-747-3016

Biblical quotations, unless otherwise noted, are from
the New Revised Standard Version of the Bible (NRSV).

*Library of Congress Cataloging-in-Publication Data*

Dempsey, Ron D.
    Faith outside the walls:
    why people don't come and why the church must listen/
    Ron D. Dempsey.
    viii + 136 pp.                                  6" x 9" (15 x 23 cm.)
    Includes bibliographical references.
    ISBN 1-57312-096-0      (alk. paper)
    1. Non-church-affiliated people—United States.
    2. Evangelistic work—United States.
    3. United States—Religion—1960-
    I. Title.
    BR526.D46      1997
    266'.022—dc21                                    97-8095
                                                         CIP

# CONTENTS

# PREFACE

My interest in the unchurched began when I started contemplating a subject for my doctoral dissertation. My mentor, Dr. Larry McSwain, suggested the unchurched as a possible topic, so I jumped at it. As I began to read what had already been written about the topic, I detected a gap in the research. Most of the literature described the demographics and descriptive elements of the unchurched. No one had measured the religiosity. So my quest began.

My journey through the lives of the unchurched turned up some very interesting experiences. I spoke with a couple of Satan worshipers and got into a few theological arguments, but mostly I found normal, everyday people who believed in God and thought faith was important in their lives. Their problem was not with Christianity, but with churches. They see churches as hindrances, out-of-date, out-of-touch, and irresponsible. Therefore, the issue is not convincing the unchurched that Christianity is the right way, but convincing them that churches can be relevant and vital in their lives.

The reader will find little theological basis for the development of the unchurched religiosity. In fact, there is nothing theological about it; it is sociological. The cultural changes in the United States have altered and shaped the religiosity of the unchurched. Therefore, when multiple sources of meaning are discussed, such discussion should not be viewed as a theological argument. Such discussion is a sociological analysis of the American culture.

I offer some scriptural support for the changes that need to occur in churches if they are to be relevant and integral in the lives of the unchurched. Most of the suggestions for churches, however, lack emphasis on "spiritual" or "theological" changes. The reason is quite blunt: the unchurched do not care. When they are looking at a church, they do not concern themselves with spiritual or theological matters. They make their decisions about churches based on very mundane, human elements. The transition from being a nonchurchgoer to being a churchgoer operates in the human realm. After the transition, the journey of spiritual and theological discipleship can begin.

This book is based on the organizing principles found in Colossians 1:9-10a. Paul wrote,

> For this reason, since the day we heard it, we have not ceased pray-ing for you and asking that you may be filled with the knowledge of God's will in all spiritual wisdom and understanding, so that you may lead lives worthy of the Lord.

The organizing principle is first knowledge, next wisdom/understanding, and then application. This principle has been helpful in my teaching (religious and nonreligious), sermon preparation and delivery, and writing.

Chapters 1 and 2 focus on knowledge and examine the cultural changes in the United States that have laid the foundation for the unchurched religiosity. I examine the processes of secularization at the cultural and institutional levels in chapter 1, and at the individual level—the privatization of religion—in chapter 2. The privatization of religion is the model for the unchurched religiosity.

Chapters 3 and 4 seek to deepen understanding about the religiosity and faith of the unchurched. In chapter 3, I examine the religious per-spectives of nonchurchgoers by exploring their characteristics, their perspectives of the church, and their reasons for leaving the church. In chapter 4, I look at the unchurched religiosity itself, which is broken down into beliefs, public and private religious behaviors, public and private consequentiality, and personal cognition. I explore the role of the church in the unchurched's religiosity and then conclude with a composite of the unchurched religiosity.

Chapters 5 and 6 offer suggestions for changes in the ways we "do" church in order to make the church more relevant in the lives of non-churchgoers. In chapter 5, I offer suggestions for changes in reaction to the unchurched religiosity itself, and in chapter 6 focus on proactive changes in churches that can help them impact and shape the religiosity of the unchurched.

# Chapter 1

# THE LANDSCAPE
# OUTSIDE THE WALLS, PART 1
## The Secularization of American Religion

John Sommerville is a lifelong Presbyterian missionary to South Korea and an alumnus of the college where I work. In 1994, he encouraged the college leadership to develop exchange relationships with the university in Korea where he taught. At one meeting, John discussed the changes he had witnessed in his forty-year tenure in South Korea. He talked about the time when he arrived to find an agricultural nation on the verge of war with its northern brothers. The Korean War had devastated the landscape. Cities were in shambles, and the government was rocked by scandal and military coups. "But now," he said, "it is much different."

I was able to visit Korea with John in the summer of 1994. As the plane descended into Seoul, South Korea, the site was spectacular. The modern city with its skyscrapers and shining buildings went on and on. As far as the eye could see, the city stretched and wound between the hilly landscape of Korea. When our group finally met up with John, he said, looking out over the countryside, "The landscape has changed a great deal."

In our world of modernization and urbanization, landscapes change very quickly. Unfortunately, many churches have been unaware of the changes in the landscapes outside their walls. For many churches, the stained glass windows and the sanctuary walls have either filtered out those landscape changes or have isolated the people inside from the changes that have occurred. If churches plan to continue to be effective in our American society, they must recognize that the landscapes outside their walls have changed.

When most people hear the word "landscape," they immediately think of the physical landscape. They see a community becoming more urban or transitioning from one ethnic group to another. Physical landscapes, however, are not the only ones that change. Mental and spiritual landscapes change as well in reaction to the very same causes of changes in the physical landscape. In this book we will examine a particular fixture of the changing spiritual landscape in our nation: the faith that exists outside the walls of the church.

As a minister, when I think of religion, the first picture that comes to my mind is my local church and its ministry. For me, that is religion—a community of believers in Jesus Christ meeting for worship and study and leaving to do ministry and evangelism in the world. Because of this very standard view of "religion" in our society, we have come to associate church attendance with religion. In fact, for many years the actual determination of religiousness was belief in God and church attendance. "Do you believe, and do you attend?" If "yes, yes" were your answers, you were religious. If "yes, no" or "no, no" were your answers, then you were not religious. If you answered "no, yes," then you were religiously confused.

So when it comes to examining these individuals who say "yes, no" or "no, no," the religious community has already interpreted their religious existence as nonexistence. Pagans, heathens, antireligious fanatics all are terms used to describe these people. The common religious research terms for these people such as apostates, nones, and dropouts depict these people as religiously antagonistic. Even the label "unchurched" has the connotation of unreligious, even antireligious because it clearly shows that such people do not fulfill the correct criteria of being religious.

The truth is, unchurched persons are not totally secularized people who give no thought to religious matters. They are definitely not antireligious freaks who burn communion cups and effigies of Baby Jesus. George Hunter reminds us that secular people "are not, by and large, areligious, immoral, or sophisticated"[1] atheists. They are normal, everyday people who get up, eat, go to work, come home, play with their kids, volunteer some free time, recreate, relax, watch TV, and sleep. In fact, many of them see themselves as being quite religious. For most of us who have our preconceived picture of religion being within the walls of the church, it is surprising to find faith outside the walls.

During my seminary days, I taught some sociology classes at the local university. One evening I was waiting outside my class, organizing my survey items for my research on the unchurched. A middle-aged female student in the class sat down beside me and asked what I was doing. After explaining my research, she launched into her religious life story. She had grown up in church, left the church during her teenage years, experienced a wild lifestyle during her college and young adult years, married, divorced, and then experienced a personal religious struggle. Now, she is comfortable with her religiousness that includes meditation, spiritual readings, and prayer.

This situation was repeated for me in various forms by numerous other persons ranging from young to old, male to female, blue collar to white collar, conservative to liberal. All told me stories of their religious lives. Many of these spiritual lives were quite vibrant and healthy, but none attended church or any other religious institution on a regular basis. Before I had even begun my research, my hypothesis that there really was faith outside the church walls was being confirmed.

## Secularization: Savior or Bane?

How can this be? How can so many people who have no connection with a local church be so obviously religious? This environment in which such religiousness can prosper has been developing in our society over the past century under the auspices of secularization. Secularization has been occurring for as long as religion has been in existence, but the past century of the United States has seen some major changes in social structures that have heightened the effects of secularization. In the 1960s and 70s, sociologists and church persons were hailing secularization as the savior or bane—depending on one's perspective—of modern society. People attributed secularization to industrialization, modernization, TV, division of labor, and countless other modern social phenomena. Most of them were right on the causes of secularization, but their definition was wrong.

Most defined secularization (in obviously more intellectual terms than this) as the death or decline of religion. Secularization was not the destruction of religion, however, but the transformation of religion. Religion adapts and transforms itself in face of such societal changes because—as Robert Lauer put it—"secularization involves a change in religion, not its disappearance."[2] Peter Berger believes that secularization ensues from a dialectical interaction between religious ideas and social changes (such as industrialization).[3] The thesis and antithesis create the synthesis of secularization, which then leads to changes in religious ideas. Berger states that this shift in consciousness does not lead to the death of religion, but just "a weakening of the plausibility of religious perceptions of reality."[4] This weakening does not take into account the development of new religious forms, but represents the faltering of the old religious worldview.

American society has created with its modern social structural changes a multifaceted religious/meaning system. What once was a straightforward, single-faceted system comprised of the traditional

Christian religion, under the pressures of American society, now has been transformed into a multifaceted system. This multifaceted system has seen not only the development of new religious movements or the inbreaking of Asian religion into the Western world, but a change in how people actually perceive religion itself.

## The Castle and the Power

Sometimes my daughter and I make up a bedtime story. We start with "once upon a time," add whatever stuffed animal she sees, incorporate her day at playschool, and then have a great story. I want to tell a story about the church and secularization that will help describe what has occurred to the church and how religion is perceived by Americans. The story tells about a "power" source. Please do not see this source as God's power. The power source relates to a functional idea of religion that provides meaning, values, beliefs, and structure to people's lives.

> *Once a upon a time a great castle sat upon a hill. The castle was surrounded by great walls, but people freely walked in and out of the castle. The walls were there to keep in the great source of power that resided in the castle. This power source offered the "meaning of life" to all who chose to partake. For centuries, the castle guarded and maintained this source of power. If people wanted to partake of the power, they had to visit the castle.*
>
> *Over the years, the castle began to decline. The walls around the castle began to age and decay until there were great gaps in the walls. There seemed to be less life in the castle, because the power was leaving it. Through the gaps, the source of power began to seep out of the castle and flow through the countryside, in the streams, the roadways, and the fields.*
>
> *Soon the power had permeated much of the surrounding landscape. People began to visit the castle less and less. Many of its crumbling walls were used to build other structures necessary to meet the needs of the people. The people even began to build other castles. The original castle lost its place of prestige. Many believed that they no longer needed to go to the castle for the "meaning of life." Now the power seemed to be everywhere. They found it in the flowers that grew along the roadway. They felt it in the surging through the waters of the stream. They harvested the power in their fields. It was as though each person had found his or her own route to the power source.*

Note, as the castle wall began to break up and the power source began to seep out, the castle did not die, nor did the power source cease to exist. They were both transformed. The power source was not "God's power." The power source is the idea of religion—where it is housed, who has access, what one does to tap in. The changes in the American mentality have removed the church as being the sole provider of religion, even the sole provider of Christianity. Americans believe that religion, and even Christianity, can be obtained from other sources. The transformation of the castle and the power source occurred at different places, each with different manifestations of the transformation.

The transformation can be categorized as secularization, and the different places can be categorized into three levels of societal change: cultural, institutional, and individual. The chart on page 12 provides a conceptual model of secularization at the different levels along with the corresponding symbols for the castle story.[5] The model includes the three levels of societal change, the processes of secularization that occur at each level, and the religious change that accompanies each process. The three levels of societal change are (1) cultural, which deals with the society as a whole; (2) institutional, which examines the organizational expression of religion; and (3) individual, which examines religion at the personal level.

## Secularization: The Cultural Level

The cultural level looks at the changes caused by secularization that are occurring at the overarching societal level. The processes at this level deal with societal values, symbols, national beliefs, and societal cohesion. The processes of secularization at the cultural level are generalization and disenchantment.

### Generalization

In her book *It Takes a Village,* Hillary Rodham Clinton discusses the validity of an old African story and its application to the modern world. She speaks of how children in the village were raised by their parents but were also exposed to other individuals in the village who aided in their care and development. She readily admits that the "village" is no longer seen in modern society. It is no longer a place; it is a network of values and relationships. These values are global values. The village has been replaced by a global community that has developed values and relationships that hold it, not just the village, together.

Generalization refers to the attempt by society to generate these common values, relationships, symbols, or ideas that may bind it together. As our society has become more pluralistic, we have had to create values and symbols that are "general" enough to bind together the different groups that comprise the American society. For years the values and symbols of the Christian faith were sufficient to hold our rather homogeneous society together. No more. With the immigration of new cultures, ethnic and religious, the United States has become the melting pot of cultures. The different cultures have not melted, however. Rather our system of values, symbols, and ideas have broadened to incorporate all the different groups. The developing variety of meaningful symbols and the ability to construct different symbol systems (generalization) lead to pluralism.[6] Generalization of the symbol system creates the problems of religious absolutism or relativism. Modern religion does not disappear but faces new challenges to its position as the ultimate source of meaning.

Richard Fenn illustrates how this generalization occurs in American religion. In the first stage, there is the separation of distinctive religious institutions. It involves a process called differentiation, which will be discussed at the institutional level. Areas of religious institutions undergo fragmentation such as the division of the clergy and laity, the development of special interest groups and denominations, and the relegation of religion to the private sphere.

In the second stage, there is a demand for clarification of boundaries between religious and secular issues. Our nation, where the civil government has established the separation of church and state, has created a legal motivation to continually scrutinize the boundaries between the religious and secular issues. Under such scrutiny, religion is not only relegated to the private sphere, but a vigilant watch is maintained to keep it there. This relegation limits religion's influence on society's meaning systems.

With religion relegated to the private sphere, the third stage requires the development of generalized beliefs and values that transcend the potential conflict between the large society and its component parts. With Christianity removed from its over-arching place as the provider of the nation's values, society must look for general concepts that can appeal to different groups.

Once the development of generalized beliefs begins, the fourth and final stage introduces emerging minority and idiosyncratic definitions of the situation. Since Christianity no longer represents the absolute truth, new claims to truth and interpretations on every situation can be made. Christianity's claim may remain dominant, but it has lost its absoluteness.[7] Secularization as generalization removes religion from its pinnacle role as the primary source of meaning and places it among competing systems of meaning. It also removes Christianity from its pinnacle role as the primary source of values and beliefs that have bound the country together. Other sources of values and beliefs can claim they offer meaning and symbols that can bind our nation together.

*Two events apply to generalization. First, seeping out of the power from the castle to the surrounding landscape symbolizes the loss of the church as the sole provider of religious and personal meaning in one's life. Now other places can lay claim to such a role. The power becomes generalized throughout the society as opposed to being specifically located in one institution, the church. Second, because of the loss of this role as the specific source of meaning, the church has become one choice among many, even among its own kind, represented by the building of other castles.*

## Disenchantment

One of my favorite legends is about King Arthur and the Knights of the Round Table. In the various retellings of the story, one author tells of an encounter between Merlin and Arthur. Arthur is asking Merlin to look into the future and tell what he sees. Merlin begins to speak about the surging influence of Christianity, which was a phenomenon of Arthur's day. Merlin laments, "The One God comes to drive out the many gods of stone and stream and wood." Merlin is telling how Christianity will drive out the superstitious religions of Arthur's day when people saw spirits and fairies in the stones and trees and rivers. Merlin was all too right about one god driving out another. In modern times, Max Weber, a classical sociologist, says that the god of rationalization has come to drive out the Christian God. Merlin's words are echoing in our ears again, but this time it is Christianity being driven out.

The disenchantment of the world refers to the loss of the transcendent or supernatural dimension in modern society. The world turns from a supernatural perception to a "this world" perception. The progression of history has witnessed the emergence of a more scientific, rational view of the world. Efficiency and pragmatism replace the supernatural and mystery of the world. The gods of rationalization and science have tried to drive out the supernatural gods. The pragmatism of the new worldview questions, if not negates, supernatural explanations and superempirical ideas. Humans turn away from transcendent causes and concentrate on temporal explanations. The supernatural loses its social significance. The world becomes a rational, humanized place, without transcendent enchantment.

Christianity as a supernatural religion suddenly finds itself in a world that supposedly has "rid" itself of its need to believe in the supernatural. The church as the proponent of this supernatural religion and defender/ herald of a supernatural savior has found it difficult to speak to this rationalistic, humanistic world.

> *The castle was once seen as the sole source of the power. Now that the power has permeated all of the landscape, the castle is no longer held in awe by the people. It has lost its "enchantment." The church no longer holds the only source for meaning and has loss much prestige due to its loss of such power.*

## Secularization: The Institutional Level

The institutional level examines American Christianity from the most common perspective, the church. The processes of secularization at the institutional level are routinization, decline, and disengagement/differentiation. These processes are gauged by changes in numbers, structures, programs, and organizational behavior.

### Routinization

Routinization is the ultimate in institutionalization. The church is a prime example of a routinized system. The church throughout its history has taken the values, beliefs, and teachings of the Christian faith and developed creeds, codes, rules, regulations, clergy, programs, and so on to the point that we have institutionalized the "meaning" out of those original values, beliefs, and teachings. "Doing church" has become a routine that has as much to do with the fact that the processes of doing church have become so institutionalized as it does with the mindset of the church attendee.

For many people, church is the ultimate habitual ritual in which they go through the motions with no thought of the original intention of what they are doing. That mindset, coupled with the institutionalized tradition of what they are doing, has created a state of routinization in the American church. Max Weber called routinization an iron cage that leads to a "mechanized petrifaction."[8] A large number of churches have become petrified in their traditions and processes and are either unaware or unwilling to admit that the world around them has changed.

*The decaying of the walls represents the routinization of church life.
Routinization has within in it the idea of lifelessness—people moving from one task to the next without any joy or spirit. Many
churches have been void of joy and spirit due to the routinization of
their church life.*

## Decline

The decline of religion actually means the decline of religious numbers,
mainly in the area of participation in religious institutions. This participation can include church attendance, membership, religious groups, and
consensus on moral issues. This picture of secularization is the most common. It creates images of closed churches and shrinking attendance.
Bryan Wilson summarized this position by defining secularization as

> the decline in the proportion of their *(individuals)* time, energy, and
> resources which men devote to superempirical concerns; the decay
> of religious institutions; the supplanting, in matters of behavior, of
> religious precepts by demands that accord with strictly technical
> criteria; and gradual replacement of a specifically religious
> consciousness.[9]

American mainline Christianity has seen significant declines in
church attendance since the 1950s. Such decline has prompted many
church leaders to declare war on modern society as the bane of Christianity. The 1980s, however, saw increases in church attendance as well as
interest in religion, especially in the charismatic and evangelical Christian
churches. Add to this the development of new religious movements and
the surge in popularity of Asian religions, and religion does not appear to
be in dramatic decline but in a process of transformation.

Churches must pay attention to the use of people's time, energy, and
resources. The last of these three, resources, has always been seen as a
commodity, mainly money. In American society today, time and energy
have become commodities. People will spend their time and energy as
carefully as they spend their money. They will spend their time and
energy on the same things they spend their money on, the things that
give them fulfillment.

*The people stopped going to the castle because they no longer felt they
needed to go. American society has decided that to be a good person
and even a good Christian, participating in the life of a local church
is not necessary because the church no longer contains the sole source
of meaning for their lives.*

## Disengagement/Differentiation

Think about your day for a minute. How many different places or institutions did you visit today? During a normal day, I will go to my children's playschool, my workplace, my church, a restaurant or two, Blockbuster Video, Wal-Mart, the YMCA, the doctor's office . . . Why do I go to all of those places? For childcare, entertainment, education, work, recreation, spiritual needs, fellowship, medical attention . . . Our worlds have become divided into specialization areas so that we have to go to a different place for our every need. At least these superstores can combine some of these places together.

The church used to be a superstore. It was the center of the community. It provided the recreation, political services, counseling, education, fellowship, spiritual needs, and sometimes even medical attention. The church has experienced differentiation and fragmentation, however. It no longer holds the central role in the lives of people. Religious institutional differentiation is the persistent removal of the various functions that once belonged to the church into different segments of social life. Differentiation has also broken down the Christian religious monopoly and confined religion to a specific social sphere. Religion now exists alongside the other social systems of economy, politics, education, and so on. Many of the functions of the church have been removed or given to other social institutions. This process of secularization also places religion in the private sphere where its influence over the public sphere becomes limited. Emile Durkheim, a classical sociologist, wrote,

> Religion tends to embrace smaller and smaller portions of social life. Originally, it pervades everything; everything social is religious. . . . Then little by little, political, economic, scientific functions free themselves from the religious functions.[10]

Religion no longer controls the major functions of the society nor is its influence as powerful as before. There has been, as Talcott Parsons described it, a "series of 'declarations of independence' from the close cultural—especially religious—'supervision.' "[11]

*The church has had many of its functions (the walls) removed to other social institutions (the other buildings) and has lost its original prestige due to the loss of these functions and to the development of other religious institutions and expressions (other castles).*

## Secularization: The Individual Level

The processes of secularization at the individual level are privatization and secularism. Privatization incorporates most of the unchurched persons today. True secularism exists minimally.

### Privatization

One of the most significant changes to the American religious landscape is the privatization of religion. This transformation of religion at the individual level has caused the most problems for traditional American Christianity, much more than any secular humanist or atheist or antireligious zealot.

> *The privatization of religion is equated with the seeping out of the power source into the highways and byways of the landscape. People no longer believe they have to seek out the castle for the power source. They believe they can find it anywhere. The decision now is in where to find it. A decision has become one of personal choice.*

### Secularism

Secularism is the total negation of any religious motivation, experience, or belief within an individual. Though the United States may appear to be filled with such people, it is not the case, at least not in the minds of individuals. A very small percentage of the American population would classify themselves as being totally secular or atheist—however you would like to term it. Most Americans see themselves as religious in some way.

## Conclusion

The privatization of religion dramatically impacts American Christianity and its churches. This process of social change receives its strength from its grounding in the American culture. Americans believe in personal choice. They believe in the privacy of the individual. They expect to have a say in where and how they choose to engage in religious activities and express their faith. Because of these beliefs, the privatization of religion has flourished. Chapter 2 expands on the idea of the privatization of religion, focusing on the foundation, pillars, and pinnacle of this social phenomenon that has changed the face of the American religious landscape.

## The Processes of Secularization and the Religious Changes

| *Level* | *Process* | *Elements* | *Changes* |
|---|---|---|---|
| **Cultural** | *Generalization* | -breakup of dominant worldview<br>-society searches for common beliefs | -civil religion<br>-pluralism |
| | *Disenchantment* | -rationalization<br>-loss of transcendence<br>-total negation of supernatural<br>-utilitarian rationalization | -supernatural religion loses social status<br>-religion must be marketed<br>-religion falters |
| **Institutional** | *Routinization* | -move toward "church" on sect-church continuum | -conformity to world beliefs are generalized<br>-pluralistic doctrine |
| | *Decline* | -marked by institutional variable<br>-social facts show decline | -organized religion loses adherents<br>-consolidation of groups |
| | *Disengagement/ Differentiation* | -rationalization<br>-causes segmentation of social structures<br>-religion confined to private sphere | -religion loses influence over public sphere |
| **Individual** | *Privatization* | -breakup of over-arching worldview<br>-ultimate meaning found in different sources<br>-social fact measured by personal religiosity | -religion confined to the private sphere<br>-pluralistic religious situations<br>-individual religious expressions |
| | *Secularism* | -total cognitive negation of religious experience<br>-agnostic/atheist | -religion falters |

## Notes

[1]George Hunter, *How to Reach Secular People* (Nashville: Abingdon Press, 1992).

[2]Robert H. Lauer, *Perspectives on Social Change*, 3d ed. (Boston: Allyn & Bacon, 1982) 320.

[3]Peter Berger, *Facing Up to Modernity: Excursions in Society, Politics, and Religion* (New York: Basic Books Inc., 1977) 128.

[4]Ibid., 78.

[5]Peter E. Glasner, *The Sociology of Secularization: A Critique of a Concept* (London: Routledge & Kegan Paul, 1977) 15-64; Karel Dobbelaere, "Secularization Theories and Sociological Paradigms: Convergence and Divergences," *Social Compass*, 31 (1984) 213-18; Karel Dobbelaere, "Some Trends in European Sociology of Religion," *Sociological Analysis*, 48 (1987) 107-37; Karel Dobbelaere, "Secularization Theories and Sociological Paradigms: A Reformulation of the Private-Public Dichotomy and the Problem of Societal Integration," *Sociological Analysis*, 46 (1985) 378-81.

[6]These symbols do not have to be religious in common thought. Nonreligious symbols can obtain a degree of sacredness when used in certain symbol systems.

[7]Richard K Fenn, *Toward a Theory of Secularization* (Ellington CT: K & R Printer, 1980) 37.

[8]Max Weber, *The Protestant Ethic and the Spirit of Capitalism*, trans. T. Parsons (New York: Charles Scribner's Sons, 1958) 182.

[9]Bryan Wilson, *Religion in Sociological Perspective* (Oxford: Oxford University Press, 1982) 149.

[10]Emile Durkheim, *Division of Labor in Society*, trans. George Simpson (Glencoe IL: The Free Press, 1949) 169.

[11]Talcott Parsons, *The System of Modern Societies* (Englewood Cliffs NJ: Prentice-Hall, 1971) 99.

Chapter

# THE LANDSCAPE
# OUTSIDE THE WALLS, PART 2
## *The Privatization of Religion*

The 1988 Gallup survey of the unchurched asked both churchgoers and nonchurchgoers if they believed a person could be a good Christian or Jew without attending a church or synagogue. The finding was astonishing: 88% of the unchurched respondents said "yes," and 67% of the churched respondents said "yes." The majority of Americans believe that a person can be a good Christian without having to attend church. This finding should be a wake-up call for the American church.

The privatization of religion is the transformation of traditional public religion, not its negation, in the same way that economic privatization has transformed but not eliminated many public economic institutions. It has changed them significantly, but it has not eliminated them or the need for them. Privatization of religion corresponds to a transformational perspective that believes religion adjusts to the changing culture by transforming itself into new structures and forms.

In premodern society, religion, mainly Christianity, operated as a sacred canopy. Christianity was the ground from which the society discovered and rooted its meaning. Christianity played many roles and incorporated many social responsibilities into its sphere of influence. It held communal control over the individual. The individual had limited or no choice when choosing a system of meaning. The processes of industrialization, capitalism, urbanization, differentiation, and privatization catalyzed the transformation of premodern society into modern society. In modern society Christianity is relegated to the private sphere by the process of differentiation. It is stripped of its public roles and responsibilities and confined to a private sphere of existence. The individual in modern society reserves the right to choose a system of meaning because the choice of a system of meaning is no longer limited or prescribed.

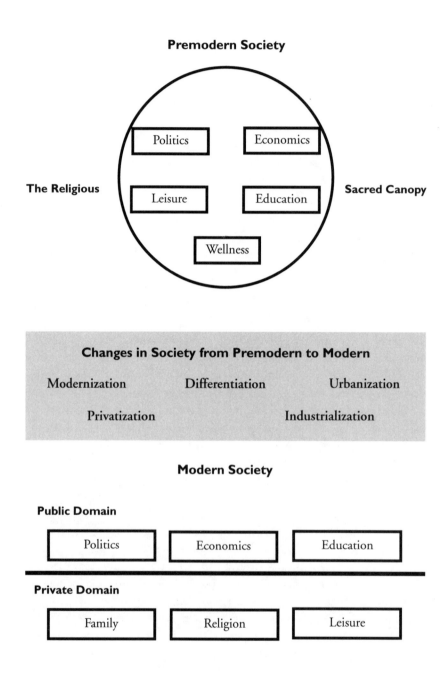

The foundation of religious privatization is the American context out of which the concept has grown. The American context contains a number of cultural patterns that allows the privatization of religion to flourish. On this American contextual foundation rests the pillars of the privatization of religion. The development of these institutional structures has provided the support necessary for the creation and legitimization of the privatization phenomenon. The pinnacle of this model is the phenomenon itself, its formation, its existence, and its essence. These three parts (foundation, pillars, and pinnacle) roughly correspond to the three levels of societal secularization: cultural, institutional, and individual respectively.

## The Foundation of the Privatization of Religion

The American context provides a fertile ground for the cultural patterns that have spawned the phenomenon of religious privatization.[1] These cultural patterns emerge from the religious, ideological, political, and economic patterns of the American context.

### Religious Patterns

The basic nature of Christianity has always been an internal idea. In the Christian history of the United States, the personalization of Christianity reaches its current zenith. The Puritans practiced a religious freedom that expressed disdain toward anyone who attempted to exert external authority. The private piety coupled with the utilitarian individualism of Lockean philosophy provided an indispensable heritage for privatization.[2] The Great Awakenings of the 1830s embraced the idea of personal belief and salvation. Charles Finney wrote:

> Now, it is strictly true, and true in the most absolute and highest sense; the act is his own act, the turning is his own turning, while God by the truth has induced him to turn; still it is strictly true that he has turned and has done it himself.[3]

This internalized element continued through the fundamentalist movement of the 1920s and into the rise of the evangelical movement of the 1940s and 50s.[4] The result of this heritage is a privatized gospel. Stephen Hart posits that a privatized gospel leads to a personalized redemption, a privatized piety, and a "salvation viewed as self-fulfillment."[5]

## Ideological Patterns

Individualism can truly be called *the* American ideology. The American society has raised the idea of the individual to almost sacred status. Eric Mount claims that "nothing is more American than individualism."[6] The structures, laws, and customs of the United States perpetuate and foster individualism. America is the only country where large masses of civilized people enjoy a surplus of unqualified individualism, unfettered by law or custom. This unqualified individualism claims such a hold on the American psyche that it lies at the very heart of the American culture.[7]

Not only does individualism have an impact upon all the public social institutions; it also affects the private social institutions, including religion. Mount describes the impact of individualism as "a kind of secular religion influencing the way they live more than the religious traditions some of them espouse."[8] Individualism not only influences American religion by impinging on its sacred space; it also changes the very practice of religion itself.

## Political Patterns

In 1778, the Constitutional Congress engraved in the fabric of America the Bill of Rights, which was to accompany the Constitution of the United Sates. The second amendment to the Bill of Rights created a formal separation between the church and the state. In doing so, the members of the Constitutional Congress were trying to avoid the tyranny of a combined religious/political system. At the same time, they formally and unknowingly set the church and religion into what can be called "the private sphere" of social life.

The public-private sphere of social life literally becomes segmented in the Constitution. Because this separation is considered a "legal" one, groups take great steps to see that it is enforced. The two issues created by this separation of church and state are (1) the relegating of religion, especially Christianity, to the private sphere of social life; and (2) the inability of religion to significantly impact the public sphere from which it has been removed.

## Economic Patterns

Two economic patterns have aided in the legitimization of the privatization of religion: the mass media and the dominance of markets in the capitalistic system. The advancement in mass media over the past three decades has increased the availability of resources for people's religious lives. Individuals can now enjoy not just religious worship services and religious instruction via the television, videotapes, and the World Wide Web; but they can get the best of these forms of religious programming. Why attend your local community church when you can hear great music from huge orchestras and choirs and listen to the most influential and popular preachers in the nation right in the comforts of your own home? Can't a person worship and learn through these mediums as well as attend their local community church? Thirty years ago such media programming was heretical. Thirty years later it is commonplace, high quality, widely accepted, and taking the place of many local community churches.

The dominance of markets in the capitalist system has thrust churches into a market game. Competition replaces prophetic witness as the name of the game. The plethora of churches has created a saturation of the market. As a church consultant for strategic and dynamic planning, I ask churches to define their target audiences because there are churches out there for every political and theological persuasion, economic status, and demographic lifestyle. Being in a market game and the plethora of churches has relativized the authority of the church. Which church is right? Which church really knows the truth? The local church cannot answer these questions because the church down the street has a different question.

*****

My grandfather laid every foundation for every building in his business. I guess he thought that if he could get the job started right, everything else would work itself out. I was always amazed as a small boy at what water and some powdery dust could do. I would watch my grandfather pour the concrete into the foundation's mold and then add water. I was amazed that at one moment I could step knee-deep into this gooey, slimy mess (which I did occasionally), and in a few hours construction workers could build a building on the same spot.

The same thing has happened to American cultural patterns. They have changed the social context of the United States, in essence laid the foundation, so that new structural and institutional changes are possible. What was not possible a few decades ago is now inevitable. On these cultural patterns are built the pillars of religious privatization.

## The Pillars of Religious Privatization

My father refuses to use an ATM card, let alone one of those debit cards. He would rather go to the bank and get the money from a teller or write a check. For many years the idea of credit cards, ATM, or debit cards was dismissed by most bankers and financiers as a ludicrous idea that would never catch on. People would never allow a number and electronic transfers to substitute for them actually handling their own money. When the idea of credit cards was first introduced, it probably *was* a ludicrous idea because structures and mechanisms for electronic transfer did not exist at the time to make those avenues of exchanging money possible. But with the advent of such inventions as computers, wire and wireless transfers, and ATM machines, the idea of exchanging money through the electronic medium became easier. Soon banks and financial institutions jumped on board, and the way to using credit cards was on the fast track. Within one generation, no one needed to be convinced that using a credit card was a ludicrous way of exchanging money.

So it is with the development of the privatization of religion. For the idea of religious privatization to become legitimate, some social structures needed to change in order to legitimate the concept. Grounded on the cultural patterns that arise from the social context of the United States are three pillars of the privatization of religion. These pillars provide the support on which the phenomenon of religious privatization rests. By support, I mean legitimization. These pillars act as the legitimators of the privatization of religion. The privatization of religion no longer remains merely an idea; it becomes a legitimate phenomenon and force in American society because of these pillars of support. The three pillars that act as the legitimator of the privatization of religion are (1) the relegation of religion to the private sphere, (2) the changing role of religion in society, and (3) privatized religious practices and beliefs.

### The Relegation of Religion to the Private Sphere

The differentiation of society has relegated religion to the private sphere of social existence. This shift from the public to the private sphere means that religion, along with other social forms such as the family, has lost much of its influence in the public sphere and becomes a choice among many even in the private sphere. One of the most damaging losses to the Christian faith has been its inability to address the needs, desires, and problems of our nation at the public level. The Christian church has been "displaced from its role as guardian of the public worldview that gives human life its coherence," as Robert Bellah said.[9] This does not mean that the Christian church cannot voice its opinions or lobby for particular causes. Rather, the effective and powerful impact of such actions at the public level has been lost. In his book, *The Naked Public Square*, Robert Neuhaus bemoans the results of this division:

> Its terrible flaw, however, is that it draws an unsustainable line between public and private. What is public and therefore the appropriate concern of the government is limited to what can be fitted into a mechanistic political process.[10]

Once this unsustainable line reduces religion to "nothing more than privatized conscience, the public square has only two actors in it—the state and the individual."[11]

In *A Culture of Disbelief*, Stephen Carter reiterates that religion has not been banned from the public arena but has lost its ability to persuade and influence in the public arena. The media and the constitutional law decisions have reduced religion's voice to one among many, which is a trivialized and sometimes shameful choice. In the 1996 presidential election, Pat Buchanan equated his religious ideals of prayer in schools, pro-life, and God and country with his political ideals of protectionism. As a result, his religious ideas were equated by the media, and thereby many Americans, with isolationism and Nazism. The relegation of religion to the private sphere has created a cultural perspective among many Americans that leads to the marginalization and trivialization of religion in the public square, heightened religious individualism, and religious privatization.

Another consequence of relegating religion to the private sphere is that religion becomes, in the words of Robert Bellah, "merely one of a variety of possible private options."[12] Even in the private sphere religion no longer holds the dominant position of offering people a source of meaning for their lives. Other choices include the family, work, friends, recreation, the arts, and community service. People garner meaning for their lives from all of these areas and will pick and choose from each as though they were selecting produce at the grocery store. Relating back to our castle illustration, the power is no longer present only in the castle; it has seeped into every nook and cranny of life, so that meaning can be found pretty much anywhere for those in the modern world.

The most important things to Harold and Sue R. are their children. Since both work, they have very few moments to spend with their three boys. Sunday provides them a time to get away or play ball or help do chores around the house. They believe that family "is the most meaning-ful expression of religion" for them at this stage of their lives. "Anyway," they exclaim, "doesn't God want us to spend time with our families?" Many times during my busy and hectic schedule, I have remembered their words and have found it hard to argue with them.

## The Changing Role of Religion in Society

The differentiation of society has stripped religion of many former responsibilities and roles. These responsibilities and roles are transferred to other social institutions, most of which continue to exist in the public sphere, such as education and health care. Most churches no longer offer general education for children, though there has been a resurgence in this area. Churches were once the primary health and social services provider in a community and also provided the recreation and leisure outlet for the community. This responsibility, however, has been farmed out to YMCAs, the county recreation department, malls, movies, and TV. So what role does religion play in the private sphere?

Robert Bellah determines that religion's main role is no longer prophetic but therapeutic:[13]

> Privatization placed religion, together with the family, in a compart-mentalized sphere that provided loving support but could no longer challenge the dominance of utilitarian values in the society at large. Indeed, to the extent that privatization succeeded, religion was in danger of becoming, like the family, "a haven in a heartless world," but one that did more than reinforce that world, by caring for its casualties, than to challenge its assumptions.[14]

Churches now offer divorce counseling, grief support groups, ministry to the aging, teen support groups, and so on. All these ministries are good and needed, but the churches are not the only ones offering such support. The local YMCA, United Way, and other public and private community services offer the same type of ministries and services. Other than the preaching of God's Word, the church does not look much different from other agencies in its community. The church that once played a very dis-tinct role in the community no longer has such a role. The church has become one choice among many.

Carol and William S. are a married couple with two children, Chelsea, age 10, and Brian, age 14. Both work at well-paying jobs. Their children are active in sports and gymnastics in their local community.

Even with a teenager like Brian, they do a lot together as a family. They go to movies, attend sporting events, and see Broadway shows at the downtown arts complex. When asked about religious activities, they said they had been to the community's Easter passion play and the large local church's singing Christmas tree and other special events. William summarized the situation in a rather sobering way:

> *We attend a lot of events in our community that are top-notch, high quality events. Most churches do not offer things like that. What they do is very mediocre. If we have a choice of attending a concert at the local auditorium or at a local church, we will choose the one at the auditorium.*

When churches held a special place in their community, they could offer mediocre programs and events. Why? Because they were the only game in town. Now churches are no more than one choice among many, and most churches are still offering programming of mediocre to low quality while the rest of the programming choices are high quality.

### Privatized Religious Practices and Beliefs

The third pillar in the privatization of religion is the legitimization of privatized religious behaviors and beliefs. Privatized religious behaviors and beliefs have always existed. Private prayers and meditation, family traditions, and religious experiences are nothing new on the religious landscape. The difference lies in their acceptance as appropriate religious activities that can be placed alongside church attendance, doctrinal beliefs, and public profession. Our social context coupled with the processes of secularization, have created the cultural situation in which such privatized religious practices and beliefs are seen as appropriate alternatives to standard public religious practices by the general society. The rules have changed. Not only do privatized religious practices and beliefs exist, but now they have become legitimized in the minds of a large majority of Americans.

A wonderful example of the legitimization of privatized practices and beliefs taken to the ultimate stage is found in *Habits of the Heart.* Robert Bellah says of the character, Sheila Larson:

Sheila Larson is a young nurse who has received a good deal of ther-
apy and who describes her faith as "Sheilaism." "I believe in God. I
am not a religious fanatic. I can't remember the last time I went to
church. My faith has carried me a long way. It's Sheilaism. Just my
own little voice."[15]

In my own survey I found no one who had taken their beliefs to such
extremes, but there were many subtle comments that hinted of such privatized belief. Not long ago Sheila would have been branded a heretic,
but now 78 percent of Americans, both in the church and outside, agree
with her.

## Privatized Religious Worldview

The pinnacle of the privatization of religion is what I call a privatized
religious worldview. In the words of Luckmann, a worldview is

> minimally actualized in the inner semantic structure of language. It
> appears to the individual as the "natural" logic in terms of which he
> [sic] perceives the world as a universe of typical things, events, and
> relations and in terms of which he orients his actions and makes his
> choices. It forms the context of all meaning in subjective experience
> . . . the crystallization of a personal perspective on the world, of an
> individual style of life.[16]

The phrase in this definition that best describes a worldview is "it forms
the context of all meaning." In essence, it is like a box made of filters that
allows certain "meaning" to enter and shape our lives. The filters will
allow certain ideas and thoughts in but not others. These filters influence
the way in which we perceive the world, thereby influencing our behaviors and reactions to certain situations. We act and react in a certain way
to situations or ideas based on our worldview. In previous societies, the
boxes did not differ much from one person to the next because most people held similar worldviews. In modern society, that is not the case. The
boxes can differ from one person to the next. We have shifted from the
development of communal, homogeneous worldviews to the development of individual, distinctive worldviews in which we have a "personal
perspective on the world, of an individual style of life."

## Formation of a Worldview

But how does a worldview get formed? It originates in human activities, mainly experiences that are at least partly institutionalized. We are socially constructed people. Much of who we are as people is dependent on our family backgrounds, family income status, parents' occupations, educational and social opportunities, plus the institutions with which we are associated. Our worldview is formed from these experiences and social structures.

The social structure in which we live transmits a reservoir of meaning, values, and beliefs that form individual worldviews from generation to generation. Worldviews are transmitted over the generations in processes that are, again, at least partly dependent on institutions. Much of our worldviews depend on certain institutions such as schools and churches and family. Conversely, social institutions depend on the continuous internalization of a worldview for their own survival.[17] Their survival depends on proper transmission of the worldview and internalization by individuals because social institutions do not transmit all of society's worldviews. With the social shift to the individual, these social institutions are transmitting less and less of the worldview.

## Formation of a Privatized Religious Worldview

How have we come to a point of developing a privatized religious worldview? We have already seen how the changes in American society have provided appropriate ideological and structural legitimization for such a worldview. Another key to its development is the decline in the churches' ability to internalize the Christian worldview into the private religious lives of people. Churches act as partial transmitters of people's worldview. They are the primary transmitters of the Christian worldview. If individuals do not internalize the worldview, then not only does the worldview of Christianity suffer, the church ceases as an institution.

Churches perpetuate themselves through the transmission of their religious worldview through the processes of socialization. Churches offer an official worldview that in turn offers meaning for life. Churches act as transmitters of the official worldview and at the same time perpetuate themselves through the successful socialization of the official worldview in the lives of individuals. For churches to continue, there must be a high percentage of socialization to the official worldview across time and generations. If a high percentage of socialization does not occur, then a gap develops between the official worldview of Christianity and the worldview of individuals. Obviously, the complete congruence does not occur; therefore, the gap between the official worldview and the individual's worldview widens.

In American society the congruence level has decreased. The complexity of relationships, the differentiation of institutions and roles, and the legitimization of religious privatization all contribute to the lessening of the congruence level. As the gap widens, the carrier of the official worldview loses its significance. Thomas Luckmann contends, "What is conceivable is that a model of religion that had been 'official' for former generations ceases to be 'official' for later generations."[18]

What fills the gap left by the declining influence and congruence of the official Christian worldview? Thomas Luckmann's early theory on privatization concluded that nonreligious systems would replace religious systems as a person's center for meaning. Some of the qualitative data suggests that family, work, and personal self-fulfillment are replacing the traditional religious system. It appears, however, that Luckmann's later theory and Robert Bellah's understanding of Christian religious persistence have the most support.

Christian symbolism survives and adapts within the modern culture even within the unchurched group. Worship styles, sacred music, educational means, and evangelistic methods all adapt over time. Other systems of meaning may have appropriated some of the functions of traditional religion in the lives of the unchurched; however, most of these persons still see a need for a supernatural element in their meaning systems. Thomas Luckmann clearly indicates that an individual's personal religious worldview begins within the traditional religious forms: "The worldview stands in dialectic relationship with the social structure. It originates in human activities that are at least partly institutionalized."[19] The unchurched may be practicing an adaptive form of spirituality that emerged as a derivative of traditional Christian religion.

The nonchurchgoing population practices a private religiosity separate from the traditional Christian institutions. Both Luckmann and Bellah indicate that a person's system of meaning can transcend the social institutions on which it may be based. The unchurched's religious meaning system does not need an institutional base on which to ground itself. Luckmann reminds us that

> the sacred cosmos of modern society no longer has one obligatory hierarchy, and it is no longer articulated as a consistent thematic whole. It consists of assortments of social reconstructions of transcendence.[20]

Most persons outside the church believe that they can develop their own religious faith without the assistance of the local church.

Another explanation for the belief that persons can develop their faith outside of the church is the emergence of individualism in society. Luckmann and Bellah believe that the rise of individualism plays a major role in the American religious scene. Bellah states that "the diversity of practice has been seen as legitimate because religion is perceived as a matter of individual choice."[21] Finding a church that fits, choosing to discover religion in private, gleaning what one thinks is right from any meaning system all indicate individualism as a major source of religious privatization among the unchurched.

Luckmann and Bellah contend that the church has fallen behind the cultural changes of modern society and now stands silent to the questions of the modern individual. Many nonchurchgoers have experimented with organized religion and found it void of meaning. Please understand, it is not that the church's message of the gospel is void of meaning. Rather, these individuals find no meaning in the way the church presents the message. They seek answers. They are searching across denominational, world religion, and humanistic lines to find a system of meaning for their lives. Yet the church still has the message, the one that can bring meaning to the unchurched. But the unchurched cannot hear it because churches are unwilling to change their religious rhetoric in order to speak to these searching individuals.

The relegation of religion to the private sphere grants new freedom to the individual. Luckmann asserts that "personal identity becomes a private phenomenon. This is, perhaps, the most revolutionary trait of modern society."[22] The liberation of individual consciousness from the social structure and the freedom in the private sphere provide the basis for a somewhat illusory sense of autonomy that characterizes the typical person in modern society. Premodern society held sway over the individual's worldview through social and religious control. The individual had no choice other than the dominant Christian worldview. Modern society allows the individual to remove himself or herself from this once-dominant religious worldview because the differentiation of society now supposedly provides the individual with multiple choices of ultimate significance.

## Conclusion

We Christians would not agree with this line of thought since Jesus is the only source of ultimate significance. The loss, however, of the church's dominating authority position has created a societal belief that an individual can arrive at his or her own system of ultimate meaning. All of our discussion leads us to this point. The processes of secularization have created in the American society the legitimate opportunity for the individual to develop and practice a privatized faith. The unchurched have embraced this opportunity. Therefore, the next two chapters examine the privatized religiosity of this group. Chapter 3 focuses on their religious perceptions, including reasons why they do not participate in church. Chapter 4 explores their faith and how the church is intertwined in that faith.

## Notes

[1]Stephen Hart, "Privatization in American Religion and Society," *Sociological Analysis*, 47 (1987) 321.

[2]C. Eric Mount, Jr., "American Individualism Reconsidered," *Review of Religious Research*, 22 (1981) 364. For further insight into the coupling between Puritan piety and Lockean individualism, see Robert Bellah, *The Broken Covenant* (New York: Seabury Press, 1975); Robert Bellah, et. al, *Habits of the Heart: Individualism and Commitment in American Life* (New York: Harper & Row, 1985) 28-51; and Robert Bellah and Phillip Hammond, *Varieties of Civil Religion* (San Francisco: Harper & Row, 1980) 7-17.

[3]Charles Finney, *Sermons on Important Subjects* (New York: John S. Taylor, 1836) 22. See also James E. Johnson, *The Life of Charles Grandison Finney* (Ann Arbor MI: University Microfilms International, 1980) 280-300.

[4]See George Marsden, *Fundamentalism and American Culture* (Oxford: Oxford University Press, 1980) 37, 71; Douglas Frank, *Less Than Conquers: How Evangelicals Entered the Twentieth Century* (Grand Rapids MI: Eerdmans, 1986) 21-25; Robert Wuthnow and Robert C. Liebman, eds., *The New Christian Right* (New York: Aldine, 1983) 16-18, 133-48, 175-79.

[5]Hart.

[6]Mount, 363.

[7]The entire subject of individualism is too extensive to discuss here. For further information, see Alexis de Tocqueville, *Democracy in America*, trans. G. Lawrence (New York: Doubleday, Anchor Books, 1969; Robert Bellah, *Habits of the Heart*, and Yehoshua Arieli, *Individualism and Nationalism in American Ideology* (Cambridge MA: Harvard University Press, 1964).

[8]Mount, 362.

[9]Robert Bellah, "Discerning Old and New Imperatives in Theological Education," *Theological Education,* 19 (1982) 12.

[10]Robert John Neuhaus, *The Naked Public Square: Religion and Democracy in America* (Grand Rapids MI: Eerdmans, 1984) 137.

[11]Ibid., 82.

[12]Bellah, "Discerning."

[13]Bellah, *Habits,* 224.

[14]Ibid., 221.

[15]Robert Bellah, quoted by Thomas Luckmann in "Religion in Modern Society: Individual Consciousness, Worldview, and Institutions," *Journal for the Scientific Study of Religion* 2 (1963): 153. For further insight into the internalization of the worldview, see 154-55.

[16]Ibid., 54.

[17]Ibid., 87.

[18]Thomas Luckmann, *The Invisible Religion* (New York: MacMillan, 1967) 61.

[19]Thomas Luckmann, "Shrinking Transcendence, Expanding Religion?" *Sociological Analysis,* 50 (1990) 134.

[20]Ibid.

[21]Bellah, *Habits,* 221.

[22]Luckmann, *The Invisible Religion,* 97.

# Chapter 3

# THROUGH A STAINED GLASS DIMLY
## *The Religious Perspective of the Unchurched*

My father refereed high school football while I was growing up. Sometimes I would go to the games with my mother and brother to watch him. My mother did not like to go because everybody yelled at my dad. During the first few games, I noticed that dad and the other referees would sometimes gather together. I finally asked my mother what they were doing. She said they were huddling to discuss the last call. My mother explained that one of the football players had done something wrong and each referee was telling what he saw so they could make the right call as a group. Multiple perspectives always provide a better picture of the situation. We will examine some religious perspectives of the unchurched in order to gain a more complete picture of who they are and their relationship to the church.

A descriptive picture of the nonchurchgoer would be a thirty-five-year-old male college graduate who has been married and divorced, is planning to marry again, resides in the West, and has had religious training during his younger years.[1] George S. has traveled this road. George grew up as a Presbyterian in the Northeast. His parents were marginal church members, but he knew "the basics" about Christianity, Jesus, and the church. When he entered a large university in the Midwest, he "took a hiatus" from religion and began experimenting with different lifestyles. This experimentation continued through his young adult years and first career job in engineering. When he married at the age of twenty-nine, he and his wife joined a local community church. George said he enjoyed the experience and made some good friends. He commented that the church was a little conservative for his taste, but he liked the pastor and wanted to be with his wife. Six years later they divorced, and again George dropped out of church. He is now thirty-eight and dating someone seriously—even though "she has a seven-year-old daughter." His present partner does not attend church, but they have been talking about it for the sake of her daughter.

George is typical of the unchurched.[2] In his story we discover several characteristics that influence their views on Christianity and the church. Some of them have one or two of these characteristics; some have a combination of several. All the characteristics provide insight into better understanding the unchurched.

## Characteristics of the Unchurched

Many persons who do not attend church have shed traditional values during a period of experimentation and rebellion. Others do not attend because of a real or perceived idea that something is wrong with them because they do not fit the role of a typical church member.

### Experimentation

Lack of relationship to the church normally begins during the college years.[3] The parental controls have been shed, and the young person also chooses to shed, for a while, the "values" of the parents. These "values" can include the traditional religious patterns of church attendance, behavioral restrictions, style of dress and appearance, and so on. Once the parental controls are gone, the young person will begin to experiment. Experimentation is a normal part of the post-adolescence experience. Religion is not immune to this experimentation stage, and so a young person's faith gets added to the experimental crucible along with everything else.

James Fowler described this stage of faith, which corresponds to the experimentation period of young adults, in the following way:

> For a genuine move to Stage 4 to occur, there must be an interruption on reliance on external sources of authority. The "tyranny of the they"—or the potential for it—must be undermined. . . . The two essential features of the emergence of Stage 4, then, are the critical distancing from one's previous assumptive value system and the emergence of an executive ego.[4]

The executive ego is associated with the movement into experimentation.

The pattern of experimentation of the unchurched does not suggest that people abandon religion or even become antireligious because they come to the conclusion that religion and faith are bad. The pattern indicates that religion and religious activities were part of a childhood dominated by parents that many young adults will give up during the experimentation time to explore new areas of experience. These new areas of experimentation include nonreligiousness, nominal religiousness, and alternative religiousness.[5] Glock and Wuthnow, who studied these areas of experimentation, found that lifestyle and environmental surroundings of the individual were the reasons for abandoning conventional religion—not the conventional religion itself. Experimentation does not lead to permanent defection. Many persons in their experimentation stage will return to conventional religion at some point.

During the beginning of the experimental stage, individuals will appear to become less religious as well as less committed to religious institutions. The apparent loss of religious faith can be tied to the psychological idea of cognitive dissonance. A cognitive conflict results when younger individuals abandon going to church. Church attendance has been so connected to their religious faith that they cannot imagine how to maintain their faith without maintaining commitment to a local congregation. So to resolve the conflict, many younger experimenters will cognitively choose temporarily "to abandon their faith." When surveyed about their religiousness or perceived faith, they will consistently have much lower rates of religiousness then older individuals. As these younger adults mature, they will again regain their faith as they begin to resolve the issue by separating church attendance from religious faith.

Howard N. grew up in a small, rural Southern Baptist church. He had active churchgoing parents who "drug him in the doors every chance they could." He was a youth leader and quite active in mission efforts and the youth choir. During his college days, "as far away from home as my car could drive," he stopped going to church. Howard says,

> *Looking back on it now, I guess it was the only way for me to rationalize not going to church. I thought I had given up my faith and turned my back on Jesus. As long as I kept telling myself that, then it was easier not to feel guilty about not going to church.*

Howard later realized that not attending church did not mean he had lost his faith. He began rediscovering his faith through scripture reading, praying, and attending Bible seminars. Howard is not back in a church, but he says, "Now I think it would be easier to go back because I know that going to church is only a part of my faith."

Experimentation lasts until the first experience of domestication, normally either permanent career choice or marriage. For most individuals, all signs of experimentation vanish when children come along. I know because I have two daughters, ages three and one. Wade Clark Roof showed that of the baby boomer crowd (largest of the current dropout groups), of the 60%–70% who dropped out during these experimental years, 24%–30% returned. Most returned due to some domesticating experience.

Not only does domestication moderate the experimentation; during the domestication stage younger individuals begin to realize that separating religious faith and church attendance does not have to lead to cognitive dissonance. People become comfortable with the idea that they can be religious. They believe they can maintain a healthy religious faith and not have to engage in the normal patterns of religious behavior.

Experimentation is an almost natural result of leaving home. The loss of parental control, the newfound freedom of time and choice all lead to the process of experimentation. Some people dabble a little and then return to a familiar lifestyle. Others have radical experiences in which their lifestyle is totally transformed from any previous experiences. Whether a person chooses either of these paths or any of the other paths in between, religious faith rarely is abandoned, but is always transformed.

### Something's Wrong

*When I attended my local church, I felt like something was wrong with me.*

At least that is how Shirley A., a middle-aged woman, described it. Shirley has been divorced twice and does not feel that her local church accepts her as a fellow member. Although she admits that no one has ever said anything to confirm this feeling and many members have been supportive during her recent divorce, still she believes the members see her differently.

Many nonchurchgoers exhibit this perspective on church life. Something in their life, normally a lifestyle characteristic, prevents them from being part of a local group of Christian believers. Divorce, singleness, and past immoral behaviors are all examples of these lifestyle characteristics. Sometimes the feeling of something being wrong is warranted. Many churches clearly express dissatisfaction with certain lifestyle characteristics both by their formal and informal social controls. Many times, the unchurched convince themselves that something is wrong. Many times this perception is maintained even when there is clear evidence that such a belief is not warranted.

**Personal Misperception.** Many unchurched have a personal misconception about the church and its reaction to a person's "wrongness." This misconception normally emerges from a person's experience with churches during the younger years. The church of the past still haunts the church of the present. Many unchurched have been personal witnesses of a church's apathy or belligerence toward a member who exhibits one of the previously mentioned attributes. They recount stories of friends or family members who have been pushed to the periphery or even out of the church because of a divorce, questionable business ventures, or suspected flaws in moral character. Such an experience proves to be extremely powerful in the development of this particular religious perspective. For some individuals, that experience is the only thing they remember about church.

Another cause for the development of this religious perspective is a slightly different variation on the same theme. Many times it is quite evident, one that is detrimental to the local church, but one that many local churches attempt to perpetuate. Persons outside the church have developed a perception of the local church as being an institution of "perfect" people. Many comment on how they watch who attends church. They believe that to attend church one has to be educated, financially comfortable, strongly grounded in traditional family values, and possess appropriate social skills. All of these attributes are, of course, relative and can vary from one social situation to another. A person making minimum wage sees the blue collar worker meeting these criteria, just as the blue collar worker sees the white collar worker in the same way. All this points to the perception that only perfect people attend church.

Churches are partially to blame for this. Promotional literature, ministry programming, and leadership roles all perpetuate the picture of the traditional mom and dad with 2.35 children who come walking (I still love that picture when we live in the day of the car) to church hand in hand. Our programming is geared toward family development that is clearly considered 2 parents with 2 or 3 children. Our leadership roles stand as monuments to those who are successful in their careers or examples of family virtues. Certainly this situation creates a dilemma. The church, however, needs to be aware of the perception such practices impart. The local church must seriously address how to properly handle this perception.

**Perceptive Perception.** As much as we would like to think differently, the reputation for excluding those who have violated some religious or social norm does not only exist in the churches of the past. A number of nonchurchgoers comment on how badly they have been treated by their local church, mainly after getting divorces. One woman spoke rather harshly about how she was excommunicated from her Catholic church because of her divorce. Her anger was genuine, and her contempt for that Catholic church of her past had spread to all churches. In a similar realm, a member of a certain congregation died of AIDS. The pastor of the church would not even preside over the funeral of the young man.

Churches must learn to separate their conviction from their compassion. We as Christians can have convictions and condemn the sin that exists in the world and in the lives of people, but we need compassion for the people, the compassion our Lord showed to those whose sin he had condemned. Because of these illustrative incidents and many more that churches have promulgated against people who have violated certain social rules, churches still have a well-deserved reputation of not wanting people who have "something wrong" with them.

## Consumerism and Individual Choice

Americans are the greatest consumers. According to Dean Hoge, our society revolves around the "production, distribution, and consumption of goods and services (including cultural ones)."[6] Religion in America is a cultural commodity. It is bought, sold, and marketed in the same way that education, health care, and Wal-Mart are bought, sold, and marketed. This is one reason why the American religious scene has maintained its vitality, unlike the British society where governmental regulations have demoralized the church's existence. Leo Pfeffer expressed well this market mentality of culture:

> Cultural competition is consistent with the American spirit. . . .
> Americans are committed to this not only in material and political
> wares, but in spiritual wares as well.[7]

Americans are the greatest consumers. Many of the unchurched, especially those looking to reengage public religious life, are the greatest of the American religious consumers. Such a mentality about consumption and the results of such a mentality create a number of issues the church must address: (1) A consumption mentality reinforces the idea that religion is a very private matter to be carried on between the individual and religious market. (2) The results of a consumption mentality are the proliferation of churches and church types. (3) Christianity is competing not only within itself, but with other social markets.

My family owns cemeteries in my hometown. Over the years this venture has grown from a plaything of my grandfather's to the family business. I am the prodigal son who is left, but my brother has stayed home and runs the sales division. The cemetery offers pre-need sales, which means a family can buy their cemetery plots, vaults, and grave markers in advance and, therefore, save on inflationary cost and unnecessary hassle at the time of death. For years and years, we offered only one kind of memorial for the gravesite—a copper-colored bronze marker (we do not allow tombstones). Clients normally would buy the cemetery plots and vaults in advance, but they rarely would buy the bronze markers until the time of death—even though it would cost more money then. We rationalized that clients did not want to buy a memorial until it was actually needed or they just did not want to spend the money at the time.

Recently, our bronze marker supplier introduced two new lines of markers, a classic line that was hunter green and a premier line that was a blended tone of pastels. They were still made of bronze and cost slightly more. My brother invested a large amount of money in a huge wall display for the new products and renovation of some office space to house them. I, of course, accused him of spending my inheritance. Pre-need sales of the bronze markers, however, went through the roof—not just the two new lines, but the old line as well. Why? Cost? Quality? Sudden philosophical change about buying one grave marker before it was needed? No. People just wanted a choice. They wanted to be able to say, "I want that, or I do not want that." It is the American way.

Religion in America is a private affair for persons both inside and outside the church. The consumption mentality of Americans contributes to the sense that the unchurched have private religious choices. They are not accountable to anyone else or to a higher authority about their religious choices. The church has no say in how they choose or do not choose to express their religious faith. My pastor cannot stand it when potential members "shop around" for churches. "Churches are not department stores," he says. I agree with his sentiments, but I disagree with his conclusion. In American society and in the eyes of the unchurched, there is little difference between a department store and a church. "Shopping around" is the way to reengage public religious life.

> *Churches are a dime a dozen in our town. We are looking for a church that is friendly and where they have good programs for the kids. In fact, whatever church they (the children) like is probably the one we will join.*

So says Richard F., who along with his wife and three children are beginning to "shop around" for a church home. Often in my writings and seminar presentations on the unchurched I am accused of little mention of God and Jesus. The previous quote is a good example of why. The unchurched do not "talk" about God and Jesus when they talk about churches. They are pragmatic people who view churches in a very pragmatic and utilitarian way. They see God and Jesus as private matters; churches are not.

To be really honest, Richard is right. The consumption mentality in American has created a proliferation of churches and church types. Small, medium-sized, large, mega; contemporary, tradition, liturgical; conservative, fundamentalist, moderate, liberal, charismatic—the variations are endless. American Christianity has responded to the American consumption mentality in a very competitive, capitalistic way. Such a development is both a bane and a blessing for Christianity. It is a blessing in that American society has one of the healthiest religious systems on the planet. It is a bane when local churches become the unchurched's shopping mall.

If competition between churches is not enough, churches are also competing against other markets for the time, money, and loyalty of those outside the church. Time and loyalty have become commodities like money. People have limited resources of time and loyalty, and so they spend them carefully on things that bring fulfillment. The consumption mentality that helped make religion a private affair has also thrown churches into a new arena of competition. Churches now face competition from the media, the entertainment sector, and the leisure/recreation arena.

Unfortunately, many churches are not able to deal with such competition. We have little problem competing with other churches that operate with approximately the same level of funds, staffing, and expertise. But this new arena of competition raises the stakes to a higher level. Because most churches operate at the level of mediocrity, when the unchurched are deciding how to spend their time and loyalty and then their money, they take into account the quality level of their choices. If churches are operating at a level of mediocrity, and then the unchurched compare that level to the quality level of media, entertainment, and leisure industries, it is not difficult to see where nonchurchgoers will choose to invest their time, money, and loyalty.

**Paradigm Difficulty**

Joel Barker, a leading business consultant, tells of the Swiss watchmakers and the invention of the quartz watch. For centuries, the Swiss were the leaders in watchmaking. They held 65% of the watchmaking market and 80% of the profits. Traditionally, they made watches with mechanical gears and bearings so that the wearer had to rewind the watch every so often. Then, a new invention occurred in watchmaking called the quartz movement watch. It did not require rewinding, had no gears or bearings, and was much more accurate than the mechanical watches. Who invented this new technology? The Swiss did. Who else? But the Swiss establishment wrote off the new invention. No one would ever buy such a watch. They were so convinced that the new technology would not sell, they did not even patent it. The new technology was picked up by the Japanese. Within a decade, the 65%-market share of the Swiss had dwindled to below 10%. The quartz watch was the watch of the future, and the Swiss were no longer the watchmakers of the world.

With this story, Joel Barker points out the importance of paradigms. Paradigms are models of thinking or ways of doing certain things. The Swiss had a certain way of making watches. Barker, however, also points out that one's paradigm can blind one to other ways of doing things. The Swiss were so involved in their own paradigm, they could not see the potential for the new quartz technology. Paradigms are powerful forces in our lives.

The church can be an obvious example of being stuck in a paradigm. But let's take a different angle on paradigms. The unchurched have a paradigm difficulty when it comes to "doing" church. This perspective is what I call "church-challenged." Many unchurched suffer from this alignment that can almost be classified as a disability. The disability is not physical or mental or emotional. The disability is one of paradigm. Persons away from the church find it difficult to reengage in a local church and then to successfully operate in it because the church operates in a different paradigm than they do. They find it difficult to deal with the church's language; knowledge base; history, heritage, and tradition; formal and informal social behavior; and spiritual matters.

**Language.** We alter our language when we enter the church. We begin to use words we have not used since last Sunday. Whether this is good or bad, we must admit that most church attendees begin to speak a new language when they enter the church domain. The unchurched do not speak the church's language. They do not understand the significance behind words such as "lost," "being saved," "salvation," "having a personal relationship with Jesus," and "deny yourself." Worse than not understanding, many times they will misinterpret the meanings. Jerry B. (a female) moaned, "All the church talks about is denying yourself. I raise four children, work seven days a week. I am tired of denying myself." We live in a world where the very language we use to describe the Christian life is a hindrance for introducing people to Jesus.

**Knowledge Base.** Even though most persons outside the church have had some previous experience in the church, normally during their childhood, they do not possess the knowledge base of the church's written foundation, the Scriptures. Due to this lack of biblical knowledge, Bible studies and discussion groups provide an awkward situation. References to names and places that speak volumes to regular churchgoers say nothing to nonchurchgoers who lack the knowledge of the story behind the name. They enter a cultural paradigm in which their bank of knowledge is limited.

**History, Heritage, and Tradition.** When I lead conferences for new pastors, I tell them that as soon as they reach their new church, they need to begin discovering the history, heritage, and traditions of the church. These three are powerful components in a church's existence. For a pastor to ignore them is suicide; to recognize them can mean access to powerful tools of motivation and change. Churches are laden with tradition and history that have bound them together through the years and are the foundations on which the future is built. It takes special effort on the pastor's part to discover the traditions and history of a church. Imagine how difficult it is for the unchurched who do not even know to look for them! Violation of tradition can lead to immediate formal or informal chastisement that quickly reminds the unchurched persons why they haven't been attending church in the first place.

A friend of mine tells the story of his first dinner with his wife's parents. He had been invited to the home of his then-fiancée for his first formal dinner with her parents, a very proper couple. The table was immaculately set with beautiful china and silverware, sparkling glasses, and brilliant bouquets of flowers. The family sat down to eat. My friend was very nervous about making any Emily Post mistakes. He placed his beautiful white napkin with the handstitched flowers on one corner in his lap and then noticed another less decorated napkin underneath. Fear gripped him. He had heard of dessert forks and salad spoons, but what was the extra napkin for? He found out soon enough, just as soon as he wiped his mouth with the handstitched napkin. A gasp came from his future mother-in-law's mouth. The father looked concerned. His fiancée informed him that the napkins had belonged to her great-great-grandmother, who handstitched them herself. They were only for decoration and were not to be used (that is what the second napkin was for). The unchurched are just as unaware of the church's tradition and heritage both universally and locally.

**Formal and Informal Social Behavior.** Closely related to tradition and history are the formal and informal social behaviors expected at church. Many times violation of these can bring swift condemnation by the church members and be very damaging to the unchurched. Even when condemnation does not occur, these persons feel awkward about their normal behavior that suddenly becomes abnormal.

My favorite example of this is what I call beer and visitation. Remember, I come from a Baptist background, but I have heard of similar experiences from my Presbyterian and Methodist friends. You are out making calls on people who have been sick or are prospective members. You enter the family room, and there sits the male of the household with a beer can in his hand. What is the first thing he does upon learning that you are a minister? Those of you who are ministers know. He tries to nonchalantly (which it never is) hide the beer can. It immediately makes him uncomfortable, and I know the visit is not going to be good. When nonchurchgoers enter a church, they feel the same way. What am I supposed to do? What I am not supposed to do? They are already off to a bad start, and they just came in the door.

> *If you want to gain a slight understanding of what the unchurched experience, attend a religious institution different from your church tradition. Visit a synagogue, a mosque, or at least a Christian denomination different from your own. Magnify your feelings about five times, and you will understand what the unchurched experience when they enter a church.*

**Dealing with Spiritual Matters.** The ultimate paradigm shift is the one between operating in a physical, rational world and then moving into a realm where spiritual matters are paramount. Regular churchgoers have a difficult time making this paradigm shift. Imagine what the unchurched experience when they have had only limited exposure to an institution that deals with spiritual matters.

The life of the unchurched is lived in the physical, mundane world. When they venture into the spiritual world or deal with the meaning of life on a personal level, the excursion is limited and infrequent. Suddenly they are confronted with a social institution that appears to have many of the physical and mundane trappings, but it is operating at a different level—the spiritual world. People, both with or without a relationship to the church, find this transition very uncomfortable. Even though the world has become a rational place, the church deals with a supernatural, otherworldly experience. This paradigm shift to an institutionalized spiritual plain is one of this most difficult for the unchurched.

## Losing Control

Why is a paradigm shift so difficult to handle? Why is it one of the greatest hindrances in keeping nonchurchgoers from reengaging with a local church? Let me offer an example. I traveled to India one summer. India is a place you do not go to vacation or to visit. You go to experience India. The sights, sounds, smells, and heat are indescribable to someone who has not experienced India. I have a videotape of the whole trip, but it is sorely lacking in reality and pales in comparison to the actual experience. I had literally left one paradigm and entered another. I was constantly uncomfortable because I was unaware of customs, appropriate behavior, and what to say and what not to say. I had lost control of my surroundings because I was no longer in a familiar paradigm.

Losing control is at the core of this paradigm shift. People who are not used to "doing church" are in the same predicament when they attend a local church as I was in India. They in essence lose control of their surroundings by leaving a familiar paradigm and entering an unfamiliar one. In India, I adjusted to the new paradigm somewhat because I had no other choice since I had to be there for a period of time. Unchurched people in the United States, however, have a choice. They do not like losing control over their surroundings, as no one would. The loss of control makes them feel uncomfortable in this new environment. Therefore, many will choose not to persist in attending church long enough to become familiar with the new paradigm.

## Lifestyle Compatibility

My wife and I went to college in North Carolina. We often traveled to the beach for spring break or after final exams. I used to love to sit on the beach and listen to Jimmy Buffet. Jimmy Buffet epitomized the perpetual beach bum. His songs told of doing nothing all day but lying on the beach, drinking, sleeping, and then doing the same thing the next day. In one of his songs he tells a little bit about himself. He sings,

> Now I'm getting old,
> and I don't wear underwear.
> I don't go to church,
> and I don't cut my hair.

Jimmy Buffet would not fit into the typical church scene.

The final and very obvious characteristic of some unchurched persons is the incompatibility of their lifestyles with the lifestyle of the church. These unchurched persons are normally younger, male, and still in their experimentation stage. Still, some within this group grow to be older adults. They are quite confident that they will never attend church even though many consider themselves to be religious. Why? The church makes them feel guilty. They are well aware of their lifestyles and the fact that such lifestyles may not be healthy, moral, or spiritual. Going to church only reminds them of this fact.

Men make up the large majority of this group. Sam H., a forty-six-year-old blue collar worker, says

> *I like to drink, I like to smoke, and I like to go out with the guys. I do all the things preachers tell you not to do. I don't really care what they think, because I enjoy doing it.*

The church itself could probably never reach such individuals through its human means. Change is only possible through prayer that Jesus will work in the lives of these people to change their hearts (and lifestyles). Only then will they be willing to adapt their lifestyles so that they are more compatible with the teachings of the church.

## Perceptions of the Church

The unchurched's perceptions of the church have changed dramatically over the past twenty years. The baby boomers in the 1970s were slowly brushing off the 60s and obviously still distrustful of institutions. They had not yet risen to the levels of power and prestige they now possess. In 1978 and 1988, the Gallup polling group conducted two major surveys on the unchurched. In 1978, the group with a church relationship (80%) displayed a great deal of confidence in the church, while a much smaller percentage of the nonchurchgoing population (38%) displayed the same confidence. In 1988, the first group remained about the same percentage (79%), while the latter increased (43%). In my research, more than 52% of the unchurched had confidence in the church.

As we move further away from the 60s, the level of confidence in the church increases. Baby boomers who were the hippies of the 60s are now the businesspeople, doctors, educators, politicians, mothers, fathers, even grandparents of the 1990s. Age and domestication always have an effect on one's perception of the church. Even the baby busters (the X generation) are much more confident in organized religion than their parents were at the same age.

Reasons for this resurgence of confidence in the church are linked to our concern for the future and a return to spirituality. The unraveling of the moral fabric, the increasing amount and magnitude of societal problems, and the realization that our strictly humanistic efforts at intervention have not worked have led to a rediscovery of the spiritual edge of life. Wade Clark Roof commented,

> Spirituality has been restored to its rightful place in the way people think, talk, act, and live. It can be argued that in its spiritual quest this generation (baby boomers), contrary to much that is said about its secularity and self-obsession, has reclaimed something fundamental to the American religious experience.[8]

The church obviously has benefited from this return to the spiritual as it is seen as a reservoir of spiritual teaching.

Recently I have been struck by the seemingly sudden interest in spirituality in mainstream America. Let me offer two examples from the popular media of this interest in spirituality. My favorite pop recording artist is Billy Joel. I have every album, tape, and CD he has produced. His album, *River of Dreams*, contains many expressions of a man who is aging and becomes aware of the important things in life. He sings a lullaby to his daughter, contemplates the end of the third millennium, and reflects on the issue of faith. In the title cut, Joel struggles with a rediscovery of faith. He sings,

> I go walking in my sleep
> from the mountains of faith to the river so deep.
> I must be looking for something,
> something sacred I lost
> but the river is wide and is too hard to cross.
> Even though I know the river is wide
> I walk down every evening and stand at the shore.
> I try to cross to the opposite side
> so I can finally find what I have been looking for.[9]

Another example of the increased interest in spirituality is the runaway number of bestselling books on the topic, for example, Scott Peck's *The Road Less Traveled*, Gail Sheehy's *Passages* and *Pathfinders*, and recently the *Celestine Prophecy*. The latter is a fictional novel about the discovery of an ancient manuscript that offers nine insights that will help humans advance to their true potentials.

I found the last several insights in the *Celestine Prophecy* to be somewhat fanciful, but I have to admit, one of the earlier insights is quite "insightful." It states that the destruction of the medieval Christian worldview by the advent of the Reformation left spiritual matters in a turmoil. During this turmoil, spiritual explorers were sent out to gain knowledge about the world and then would return to present their findings to humankind. The explorers, however, were gone longer than expected because the spiritual cosmos was expansive and complex. While the world waited, it began to latch on to the things that were available, mainly the emerging rational, scientific way of thinking. That "thinking" has dominated the world for the past 400 years. Now, says the author, the spiritual explorers have started to return, and the world has begun to again migrate toward spirituality.

Though the church may benefit from a return to the spiritual, the unchurched still have their questions about the church. The following chart shows areas of criticism of the church by this group.

### Responses of Unchurched Persons to Questions Concerning Religious Institutions

| | 1978 | 1988 | 1993 |
|---|---|---|---|
| Most churches and synagogues have lost the real spiritual part of religion | 60 | 62 | 64 |
| Most churches and synagogues are not effective in helping people find meaning in life. | 49 | 52 | 55 |
| The rules about morality preached by the churches and synagogues are too restrictive. | 35 | 32 | 28 |

Source: George Gallup, *The Unchurched American* (Princeton: The Princeton Religious Research Center, 1978) 32; personal research.

The return to spirituality has created not only a surge in confidence in the church, but has also heightened criticism of it. The unchurched are obviously looking to the church for spiritual guidance, and yet many find the churches lacking. Their search for meaning is strong. Now due to the breakup of the spiritual monopoly of the church, the unchurched believe that they have more choices of sources for meaning.

Sources of meaning in the modern world include other world and Eastern religions, New Age, family, and career. People no longer look solely to the Christian faith as their only source of meaning. Since the unchurched believe that they now have a choice of sources for meaning, they have been more critical of the once primary source, the church.

It is interesting to note that although the unchurched are critical about the church's lack of spiritual guidance, they have become less concerned about a perceived narrowness of the church's morality. This may be largely due to the recent conservative turn in the American society. Another interesting note is that the unchurched's criticism has dissipated over the idea that the church is too concerned about money. The church has either softened its push for money, or the unchurched no longer see the push for stewardship as an evil preoccupation of the church.

## Why the Unchurched Leave

Most nonchurchgoers have been involved in a local church at some time in their lives, normally during their childhood and adolescent years. Perceptions of the church are largely based on personal experiences with a particular church as opposed to the church in general. Russell Hale, whom I quote extensively in this section, provides an excellent summary of these perceptions of the church as they relate to why do not attend church. His research on the unchurched in America consisted of personal one-on-one interviews, thus making his research style qualitative. Such was the purpose of his study, not to quantify the unchurched but to paint a picture of them using their own words, thoughts, and reflections. In allowing for this sample to express their feelings concerning organized religion, the present research has attempted the same qualitative research. Therefore, a connection can be made between the findings of the present study and Hale's categories.

### Categories and Subdivisions of the Unchurched

**The Anti-Institutionalists.** Common among the unchurched are the Anti-institutionalists. This category includes those persons who are "defectors from the church"[10] due to their perception of the church's "preoccupation with its own self-maintenance."[11] These people were once loyal churchgoers. They were leaders in the church, but by being insiders, they saw too much. They express distress over the energy and time the church spent on raising money, hiring staff, and increasing its own public image as opposed to service, ministry, and evangelism. Many of them express concern that the religious institutions have turned inward. The Anti-institutionalists accuse churches of being too concerned with money, materialism, and maintenance. They also promote a privatized religion that does not need institutionalized exhibition.

**The Boxed In.** Surprisingly, not as many of the unchurched fall under Hale's category of the Boxed In. The Boxed In are persons who were church members but left the church because they felt restrained and constricted. There are three subdivisions of the Boxed In: the Constrained, the Thwarted, and the Independents, with the last two divisions having the greatest numbers.

*The Constrained* consists of those former churchgoers who felt the doctrines and morality of the church were smothering them. Very few unchurched persons fit into this subdivision who feel that churches teach a morality that constrained their lifestyles.

*The Thwarted* actually see the church as disrupting their movement toward maturity. They see local churches as either hindrances to their faith or offering no meaning for their lives. The feeling that they "were stifled, arrested in the stage of growth"[12] is common among these persons.

*The Independents* in Hale's study felt the church limited the "freedom for them to 'do their own thing' or to 'do it my way.' "[13] The present study's Independents approach their independence from a less direct angle. They exert their independence by expressing the belief that they can be religious individuals without attending a religious institution. None of the unchurched surveyed expressed a "do it my own way" independence.

**The Burned Out.** The Burned Out group also consists mostly of former church members who "tell of energies that have been utterly consumed by the church."[14] This consumption has been in the form of time, talents, and resources. The subdivisions of the Burned Out are the Used and the Light Travelers.

The *Used* are those church leaders who did 80% of the church's work. These are the folks who chair the church board, teach a Bible study, serve on the grounds committee, work in the soup kitchen, and serve Wednesday night supper—year after year. The church finally sucks every ounce of strength from them, and they can stay no longer.

The *Light Travelers* see the church as baggage they have carried so their children would have proper religious training. As soon as the empty nest syndrome comes, the church baggage is thrown off. (Personally, I include Category #7, the Nomads, with this group and the next group, The Floaters.)

**The Floaters.** The Floaters are the fringe members of a congregation. These individuals are never involved in any of the ministries of the church except worship. They come as spectators, wishing to remain anonymous figures.

There are two subdivisions of Floaters. *The Apathetic* come to church because of the expectations of some spouse or relative. The *Marginal* are those churchgoers who are afraid of responsibility so they cannot involve themselves to the point of being asked to serve.

**The Hedonists.** The Hedonists are normally a younger crowd, the early baby boomers (Hale's research and writing were done during the 1970s). The church and its relentless activities and demands are intrusions on the lives of this group. This group could easily fall into the experimental characteristic mentioned earlier.

**The Locked Out.** A number of unchurched persons are captured in the Locked Out category. Churches exclude this group, so they are labeled the Locked Out. This exclusion occurs through formal or informal excommunication, neglect, discrimination, or ignorance. Subdivisions include the Rejected, the Neglected, and the Discriminated, of which the first is the majority.

*The Rejected* have had religious institutions "close their doors against them, via formal excommunication, slight, disregard, or discrimination, overt or covert. For various reasons they believe the churches do not want them inside."[15] The Rejected consist of former churchgoers who have been pushed aside for some social or moral transgression such as divorce or infidelity. This subdivision corresponds to the unchurched characteristic that "something is wrong" with them. The unchurched develop a perceived feeling or actual response that insinuates a church does not want them.

The *Neglected* are those constituents whom the church's ministry does not address. Single parents, single adults, the poor, and the elderly fall into this group. Even moreso, the *Discriminated* are those groups of people who experience "overt acts of prejudice against them,"[16] for instance, homosexuals and AIDS patients.

**The Pilgrims.** A surprisingly large number of the study's unchurched persons can be labeled the Pilgrims and are associated with the group popularly known as Seekers. The Pilgrims are the real seekers. Their spirituality is in the process of formation, and any new religious experience draws them in. "They are on an ideological pilgrimage, searching for satisfying meanings and values."[17] Seekers have become a large group with the maturing of the baby boomers. The spirituality interests are high, yet they are not discriminating as to what spiritual path they follow. They leave the church to follow a new spiritual course. The rise in popularity of the Far Eastern religions and New Age can be attributed to this growing group. The unchurched claim they have not found a local religious body that "meets their needs" or "answers their questions." Therefore, they have developed their own ideas about God and faith that have diverged from the standard orthodox ideology. Communication with the traditional views is possible, but the Pilgrims are not able to constantly point out the "discrepancies between profession and performance"[18] of those inside the church.

**The Publicans.** To Hale, the Publicans "constitute by far the largest group of the unchurched."[19] The Publicans in the present study do not account for the largest group of unchurched, but they do account for a large number. This group sees the church as full of hypocrites. They have developed negative feelings toward the church normally due to some adverse encounter at a church. They constantly point out the "discrepancies between profession and performance"[20] of those inside the church. They view the church as being filled with hypocrites both at the lay and clergy levels. Hale's description of the Publican category suggests that his interviewees labeled the members in the local churches as "hypocrites, phonies, fakers."[21] The unchurched in the present study aimed their criticism of hypocrisy at the institutional religious leaders and the institutions in general. No one stated that the members of the local body were hypocrites. The recent escalation of scandalous religious leaders and televangelists has transferred the focus of people's criticism from the pew to the pulpit.

**The True Unbelievers.** Hale found very few "authentic unbelievers."[22] The present study found the same. Of 420 unchurched persons, only 23 labeled themselves nonreligious. Only 2 of the 23 responded to the open-ended question concerning their reason for not attending a religious institutions. One of the responders wrote of God "being her own will." Such comments correspond to Hale's description of this group as people "who embrace worldliness, in the sense that the dignity or worth of people lies in their capacity from self-realization through reason, without the benefit of supernatural revelation, of clergy, and or church."[23]

The True Unbelievers are divided into three subdivisions. The *Agnostics-Atheists* believe in no God, the *Deists-Rationalists* believe in the god of human reason, and the *Humanists-Secularists* believe in the god of human potential.

## Time Constraints

The most popular reason for not attending local religious institutions cannot be placed in one of Hale's categories. Most of the unchurched do not attend because they do not have the time. These individuals are not hedonists; they are strapped by work, family, school, and many activities modern society creates. Here we see not so much a definite reason as a constraint. The differentiation of modern society and the corresponding explosion of opportunities and choices have placed an external yet self-inflicted constraint on the lifestyles of Americans. Church attendance becomes one choice among many. When the choice includes opportunities that improve the economic situation of an individual (such as work and school), the church loses in favor of financial building opportunities. A new category needs to be created to include those individuals who are constrained by the choices placed on them by modern society.

## The Case of Young Adults

The experimentation and lifestyle choices explain the large proportion of the young adult exodus from the church. In Kirk Hadaway's study of apostates (his term for the unchurched), he wrote, "All have been influenced by counterculture values, and all have apparently rejected the church largely on the basis of value and lifestyle incompatibilities."[24] He concluded that apostasy is not always a matter of unbelief. Instead, it reflects in an individual's life choices.

Young adults also exit the church because it cannot provide meaning for their lives. Some even say that the church actually hinders their spiritual growth. Their experimentation is not with alternative lifestyles or irreligious lifestyles; their experimentation is spiritual. As a result, Far Eastern religions and New Age in the U.S. are heavily populated with young people.

### The Case of Older Adults

When older adults leave the church, the reasons become more diverse. Older adults have wrestled with the issue of leaving to a great extent because they find it harder to break away. Therefore, the reasons for leaving are more numerous and more developed. The three top reasons for their leaving are loss of meaning, dissatisfaction with community, and other opportunities.

**Loss of Meaning.** Many older adults drop out of church because the church no longer contains meaning for them.[25] This loss of meaning is normally associated with the empty nest syndrome, which signifies the changing of relationships. Parents cease to be caregivers to children who now look to others for that care. Because of these changing relationships, a high percentage of divorces occur during the empty nest syndrome. The relationship to the church is no different. The children have left home, and suddenly for many parents, their primary reason for attending church has vanished. This time creates deep struggles within the empty nesters. They must wrestle with their faith and what the church offers their faith. The results of this internal struggle manifest themselves in two ways: disassociation with the church or a faith journey.

Many older individuals discover that they have no connection with the church outside of their children's association. They never progressed beyond that level of association. So when the children are gone, then so is the need for association. They look deep into what they thought was there and find nothing.

Many older individuals will begin a faith journey. This faith journey can be as simple as looking for other churches but as complex as experimenting with new faiths. The journey, however it manifests itself, connects back to the reality that the local church these individuals have been attending cannot fulfill the need for meaning in their lives. Unlike the younger unchurched, the older unchurched do not believe the church is hindering their religious faith. They are merely struggling with what faith they do have.

**Dissatisfaction with the Community.** A large majority of older nonchurchgoers have abandoned the church because they became dissatisfied with the community rather than with their religious identification. Two types of dissatisfaction exist: genuine dissatisfaction and excuse dissatisfaction.

Genuine dissatisfaction results from a situation in the church that normally is tied to theological beliefs or interpersonal relationships. The election of women deacons in a Southern Baptist church has created genuine dissatisfaction among many members of those congregations. Differences in theological beliefs create genuine dissatisfaction and can cause the exodus of the dissatisfied ones. Some disruptions in interpersonal relationships can cause genuine dissatisfaction.

Though most interpersonal disruptions are tied to excuse dissatisfaction, some interpersonal disruptions can lead to genuine dissatisfaction. These situations normally arise between the pastor and the layperson and are associated with intense personality conflicts or the breaking of trust. Those individuals who have genuine dissatisfaction with the church do not normally leave the church completely. They will reconnect with another congregation.

Most pastors have experienced members who have excuse dissatisfaction. A couple is hurt in some way by another member of the church (normally the hurtful situation has nothing to do with the church), and so the couple leaves the church. Every time the pastor visits, the couple uses the same excuse for why they are not attending. They, of course, have not joined another church nor plan to go to another. They are only looking for an excuse not to attend any church.

**Other Opportunities.** Dissatisfaction with the church and loss of meaning have long been reasons for church exodus of older adults. A new reason has arisen in the past two decades: other opportunities. This reason for leaving connects to the consumer characteristic of the unchurched. A myriad of opportunities have emerged over the past two decades that compete for the time, money, and loyalty of this group. Nonchurchgoers (and churchgoers) now see these opportunities as a Wal-Mart shopping aisle, and their week is the cart. One older male said,

> *It's not like I don't think church is important. I do, but there doesn't seem to be any way to fit it into my schedule.*

Since older adults have struggled more with the decision to abandon the church, they will be less likely to reengage in church life than younger adults. As young adults age, they attribute their abandonment of the church to immaturity or the experimentation stage of their life. The church must work extra hard to recapture the commitments of older adults who have left.

## Conclusion

The characteristics of the unchurched and their perceptions about the church offer an excellent framework in which to place their religiosity. It is within this framework of characteristics and perceptions that the unchurched have worked out their religious faith. This framework has shaped and molded their religiosity. Therefore, this framework should be viewed as an integral part of the unchurched's religiosity.

## Notes

[1]Dean Hoge, *Converts, Dropouts and Returnees: A Study of Religious Change Among Catholics* (New York: Pilgrim Press, 1981) 96. Men (46%); those ages 30–49 (47%); Westerners (55%); college graduates (46%); the divorced, separated, and widowed (46%); and those in mixed marriages (54%).

[2]See George Gallup, *The Unchurched American* (Princeton NJ: The Princeton Religous Research Center, 1978) and *The Unchurched: 10 Years Later*; and David Roozen, *The Churched and Unchurched* (Washington DC: The Glenmary Research Center, 1978).

[3]Hoge, 96.

[4]James Fowler, *Stages of Faith: The Psychology of Human Development and the Quest for Meaning* (San Francisco: Harper & Row, 1976) 179.

[5]Charles Y. Glock and Robert Wuthnow, "Departures from Conventional Religion: The Nominally Religious, the Nonreligious, and the Alternatively Religious," in *The Religious Dimension: New Directions in Quantitative Research*, ed. R. Wuthnow (New York: Academic Press, 1979).

[6]Hoge, 96.

[7]Leo Pfeffer, *Creeds in Competition* (New York: Harper, 1958) 15.

[8]Wade Clark Roof, *A Generation of Seekers* (San Francisco: Harper, 1994) 243.

[9]Billy Joel, "River of Dreams," Columbia Records, 1993.

[10]J. Russell Hale, *The Unchurched: Who They Are and Why They Stay Away* (San Francisco: Harper & Row, 1977) 100.

[11]Ibid.

[12]Ibid., 101.

[13]Ibid., 102.
[14]Ibid.
[15]Ibid., 104.
[16]Ibid., 106
[17]Ibid.
[18]Ibid.
[19]Ibid.
[20]Ibid., 107.
[21]Ibid.
[22]Ibid.
[23]Ibid.
[24]C. Kirk Hadaway, "Identifying American Apostasy: A Cluster Analysis," *Journal for the Scientific Study of Religion,* 28 (1989) 213.
[25]Hoge, 86.

Chapter

# THE FAITH OUTSIDE THE WALLS
## *The Religiosity of the Unchurched*

JFaith, rather than belief or religion, is the most fundamental category in the human quest for relation to transcendence. Faith, it appears, is a universal feature of human living, recognizably similar everywhere despite the remarkable variety of forms and contents of religious practice and belief. Each of the major religious traditions studied speaks about faith in ways that make the same phenomenon visible. In each and all, faith involves an alignment of the will, a resting of the heart, in accordance with a vision of transcendent value and power, one's ultimate concern. Faith, classically understood, is not a separate dimension of life, a compartmentalized specialty. Faith is an orientation of the total person, giving purpose and goal to one's hopes and strivings, thoughts and actions. The unity and recognizability of faith, despite the myriad variants of religious beliefs, support the struggle to maintain and develop a theory of religious relativity in which the religions—and the faith they evoke and shape—are seen as relative apprehensions of our relatedness to that which is universal.[1]

James Fowler
*Stages of Faith*

Faith has become larger than religion. Though religion still plays a major part in faith formation, faith is not limited to religious expression. Because it is developed from many sources of meaning, faith is alive and well in society and among the unchurched. Faith truly is "the resting of the heart," "one's ultimate concern."

Before the 1960s, in the United States, measuring someone's faith or religiosity was easy: You just asked them if they believed in God and went to a church. If they said yes to both questions, then they were religious. If they said yes to one question, they were suspect. If they said no to both questions, they were an atheist or apostate. Religiosity, of course, is more complex than a mere belief in God and church attendance. As inquiries into the religiosity of persons increased, so did the ways of measuring that faith. Social researchers opted for a multidimensional approach.[2] These dimensions examined a person's faith from a number of different angles: public versus private, behavior versus cognition, belief versus action. These dimensions of religiosity include ritual behavior, consequentiality, beliefs, and cognition. All but cognition can be divided into a public focus and a private focus.

### Dimensions of Religiosity

|  | *Public* | *Private* |
|---|---|---|
| **Ritual Behavior** | -church attendance<br>-participation in parareligious organizations | -prayer<br>-scripture reading<br>-meditation |
| **Consequentiality** | -discuss religion with coworkers<br>-faith affects social behavior at work<br>-political voting | -discuss religion with family and friends<br>-faith affects behavior at home |
| **Beliefs** | -civil religion | -personal religious beliefs about God, Jesus, etc. |
| **Cognition** | -not applicable | -religious experiences<br>-religious feelings<br>-healthiness of faith |

Public ritual/religious behavior deals with someone's participation in or with a religious institution. Are they a member of a church? Do they attend regularly? Are they connected with any parachurch organizations such as Fellowship of Christian Athletes (FCA), Inter-Varsity, the YMCA, and so on? Public consequentiality examines the public consequences of a person's religious faith. Does one's religious faith affect they way they interact with colleagues at work? Does it affect their political views and voting patterns? Does it motivate them to be involved in social activism? Public belief addresses the issue of civil religion and is not a concern of this book.

Private religious behavior concentrates on actions of prayer, scripture reading, meditation, and soul searching. The amount of time spent in these devotional habits is significant. Private consequentiality probes the effect of someone's faith on their personal lives. Does it affect the way they interact with family and friends? Does it determine what they choose to engage in for leisure activities or what they watch on TV? Private beliefs address issues of belief in God, Jesus as Son of God, resurrection, and so on. Private religious cognition concentrates on the personal feelings of the unchurched. Have they had a religious experience? Do they think of themselves as being religious? Is religion important in their lives?

## The Faith of the Unchurched

The faith of the unchurched is examined using each of the religious dimensions. In order to give a broader picture of the unchurched and their religiosity, I will present data from the 1978 and 1988 Gallup survey of the unchurched as well as my own research. Graphic representations will display the responses of churched and unchurched persons from the 1978 and 1988 Gallup surveys of the unchurched and my 1993 research. The Gallup information is offered only as comparison. My 1993 study was limited to the Southern region of the United States and cannot be generalized to the nation as the Gallup study information can.

The public religious dimensions are examined first, followed by the private dimensions and beliefs. Obviously, the unchurched will show little religiosity in the public dimensions. They, however, show marked increases as we examine the private dimensions and Christian beliefs. Please note as well the differences between the responses of both groups on each dimension.

### Public Ritual Behavior and Consequentiality

As one would expect, the unchurched did not rate high on the public ritual behavior scale. It even appears that they do not engage in parachurch organizations such as Fellowship of Christian Athletes, InterVarsity, or religious seminars. They do participate in the YMCA, but many are unaware of the Christian connection with the YMCA. A recent Barna poll found that there has been a dramatic falloff in church attendance by the population as a whole. George Barna found that only 37% of Americans attend church on a given weekend, which is a decrease in attendance from only five years ago.

The faith of the unchurched does little to affect their public consequentiality either. According to the survey, their faith does not affect their behavior at work or their interaction with co-workers. They seldom discuss religion in the public arena. They feel uneasy talking about religion with people with whom they do not have a close relationship. Josie M. said,

> *Religion is an intimate thing. It is not something you feel like sharing yourself, and if you do, then you feel like you are intruding on the other person.*

It is interesting to note that the group with a church relationship showed a significant drop from public participation to public consequentiality. Many of this group had the same reservations about demonstrating and talking about their faith in the public arena.

### Public Religiosity
(Means measured on a scale of 1 to 5 with 5 as highest)

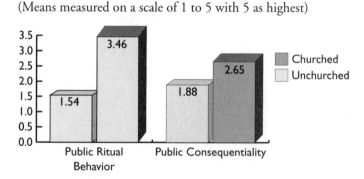

Political voting is the one area impacted by the faith of nonchurchgoers (and churchgoers). The rise of the voting power of the Moral Majority, even though people may not vote according to the Moral Majority's stance, has influenced what people consider when voting. Faith has now become a consideration in voting behavior.

### Voting behavior is influenced by religious faith

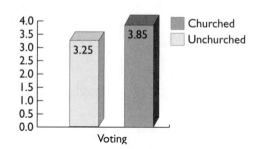

## Private Religious Behavior

The unchurched show a significant increase in religiousness when they enter the private arena. All scales increase, including behavior and consequentiality. The most important private religious behavior for all groups is prayer. Prayer is very important to many of the unchurched because it can take many forms and is between God and the individual. It is the only mechanism that places them in touch with their Creator without the trappings of other religious activities or the involvement of other people. Since prayer is the ultimate private religious behavior, we cannot judge the quality of a person's prayer. We do know that nonchurchgoers pray regularly.

Other private religious behavior takes a distant second to prayer. Nonchurchgoers are not in the habit of reading scripture, but then neither are churchgoers. The latter are much more likely to read religious books or literature, though the unchurched are more likely to read this type of literature than the Bible. In his 1996 survey, George Barna reported that this lack of scripture reading continues. He found that the percentage of adults who read the Bible weekly fell from 47% in 1992 to 34% in 1996.

An interesting trend that emerged in the interviews with the unchurched is the role of the visual media. Most persons surveyed in both groups indicated they would like to see more religious-oriented movies or videos produced. They buy for their children videos of Bible stories or that teach spiritual and moral truths. Many nonchurchgoers are as eager for the moral and religious teachings of Jesus and the Bible as are churchgoers. They just want it presented in a visual format—personally so would I.

## Private Consequentiality

The unchurched show an increase from public consequentiality to private consequentiality, but it still does not indicate an "on fire for Jesus" impact. They are more likely to let their religious faith affect their behavior with family at home. Their religious faith is less likely to impact their dealing with their friends or their leisure time choices. Nonchurchgoers, as well as churchgoers, still have a difficult time discussing religion even with their family and friends, even though Christianity strongly influences their behavior with their family and moderately influences their behavior with their friends.

One reason for this unwillingness to discuss one's faith can be gleaned from the comment by Josie M. that "religion is an intimate thing" and the importance of prayer is the unchurched's main expression of religious behavior. Religious faith is not only a private matter; it is an internal one. Not only does the religious faith of the unchurched operate significantly in the private arena of their lives; it also operates mostly on an internal behavioral level. The decision to behave in one way or the other is an internal decision. One does not normally consult another when making decisions about social interactions or proper topics of conversation or how they should resolve a disagreement with their spouse. Those situations are internal matters. Many of the unchurched say that their religious faith influences those behaviors. When it come to an externalization of that faith in the form of conversation, expression, or verbal support, these persons fall silent. They are not willing, or perhaps able, to translate their internal faith to an external one.

George Barna concludes that people both with and without a church background lack the basic knowledge and principles of the Christian faith. Hence, they are unwilling to express their faith externally. Some possible reasons for the lack of knowledge about one's faith or the fear of articulating one's faith are: (1) Pastors indirectly impose the idea that one must have a seminary degree to adequately articulate the Christian faith. (2) Pastors indirectly set standards of articulation that are too high. (3) Most persons lack basic knowledge and understanding of their faith to feel comfortable in conversation about it.

### Private Religious Cognition

"Does religion play an important role in your life?" "Yes!" cry the unchurched. Private religious cognition rated the highest of all religious scales among this group. In the minds of the unchurched their faith takes on its fullest expression, mainly because their cognitive processes are the most private, internal part of their lives.

**Importance.** The majority of the unchurched state that religion is very or fairly important in their lives. This is the ultimate expression of a privatized religious faith. The unchurched exhibit an internally strong and vital faith, but one that rarely expresses itself in public behavior. The majority believe that religion is a necessary part of their lives and is especially important because it answers many questions about the meaning of life. Is this belief in the importance of religion personally or culturally motivated? We may never know, but churches still must recognize that nonchurchgoers believe in the importance of religion in their lives.

**Importance of religion in the lives of the unchurched**

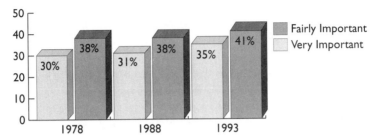

**Identification.** The unchurched in America demonstrate a strong identification with religion and mainly with Christianity. Again, one could speculate whether such identification is personal or cultural. Either way, Americans rarely will identify themselves as not religious. In the South, such identification extends beyond association with a religion group to association with a religion institution.

I live in a small town in South Carolina. Outreach and visitation in a small town is very difficult. "What?!" cry the ministers in the large urban areas, "Everybody knows everybody else. How can outreach and visitation be difficult?" Well, it is because . . . everybody knows everybody else. There are no unchurched persons in my town, at least, not any whom people know. One of the first questions you are asked in my town is, "Where do you go to church?" Of the hundreds of people I have asked this question, everyone is a member of some church. They may not have darkened the doors of that church in a decade, but they are still members. They still identify with the church normally due to some familial relationship or childhood experience. "My entire family is a member of that church," or "I was baptized in the pond out back," or "I was the first to be sprinkled in the new sanctuary." Some people who were members of my church but have not attended in years have even spoken fondly and intimately about the church and what it means to them.

This strong identification with religious faith is supported in the unchurched's designation of religious preference:

•5.5% labeled themselves as not religious.
•69.8% called themselves Christians.
•15.5% said that they were religious with no preference.

Most studies indicate that only a small percentage of Americans consider themselves atheists or agnostics. The majority of Americans identify with a particular religious faith, Christianity being the primary one. Whether or not they are active within a particular religious tradition is another question. Still, many nonchurchgoers strongly identify with Christianity, and many consider church membership important.

**Spiritual Growth.** Another interesting discovery is the concern of the unchurched about spiritual growth. They believe that spiritual growth is necessary and that they should try to incorporate such growth into their lives. They are struggling with this need for spiritual growth, however. When asked if they are satisfied with their present religious life, most answer in the negative.

Lauren T. struggles with her stagnant religious life. Her life is filled with work, marriage, taking care of two children, and going to night school. She exclaims,

> *There is no energy left in me to grow spiritually. I cry about it. I start to do something about it. I then get distracted by something else, and I cry again. I want to grow, but I just can't.*

Churchgoers are far more satisfied with their present religious lives than nonchurchgoers. The combination of the need for growth and yet the apparent lack of religious behavior in the lives of the unchurched leaves them with dissatisfied feelings about their religious lives. Such a result offers a glimmer of hope that belief and behavior are not totally bifurcated in their character. Such dissatisfied feelings are also fertile ground for churches to help the unchurched with their spiritual growth.

### Beliefs

Nonchurchgoers have always demonstrated a strong set of orthodox Christian beliefs, and, over the past two decades, an increasing number of them have adopted those beliefs. The graphs represent the percentage of persons who adhere to a particular Christian belief. We will examine the unchurched religiosity using these different dimensions. The graphs display the responses of churched and unchurched persons from the 1978 and 1988 Gallup surveys of the unchurched as well as my 1993 research. The Gallup information is offered only as comparison. My 1993 study was limited to the Southern region of United States and cannot be generalized to the entire nation as the Gallup study information can.

The number of nonchurchgoers who believe in God has always been high, ranging from 94% to 97%. A good majority of them believe that

**Persons who feel a strong need
to continue growing in understanding of their faith**

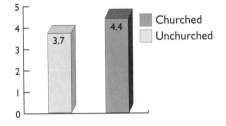

**"Are you satisfied with your present religious life?"**

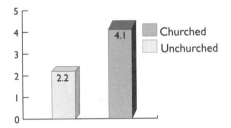

**How often do you try to grow
spiritually or in understanding of your faith?**

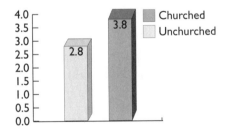

the Bible is the actual or inspired Word of God. The number who believe that Jesus is God or the Son of God as opposed to just another religious figure or a fake has increased dramatically from 1978 to 1988 and shows even more increase in the 1993 study. This statistic does not mean that they have a personal relationship with Jesus Christ or believe that they should. It does demonstrate that the gap between the unchurched and the churched on crucial Christian beliefs is not expansive. The gap is a bit larger concerning the topics of life after death and the resurrection of Jesus. The number of unchurched who believe in life after death and the resurrection of Jesus has increased only slightly over the past two decades.

Even with only a slight increase in these two topics, all of the questions on Christian beliefs showed increases in the number of unchurched who adhere to them. This rise in Christian orthodoxy among the unchurched can mostly be attributed to the aging of the baby boomers. As this large and previously rebellious crowd begins to enter their fifties, their beliefs about Christianity begin to take on a more traditional tint.

**Percentage of persons who said**
**the Bible was the actual or inspired Word of God**

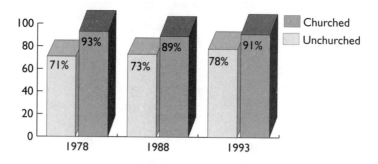

**Percentage of persons who said**
**that Jesus was God or the Son of God**

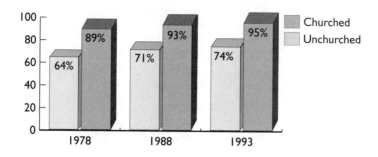

**Percentage of persons
who believe in life after death**

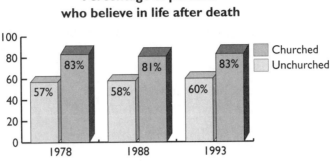

**Percentage of persons
who believe in the resurrection of Jesus**
(Note: the Gallup survey did not ask the question in 1988)

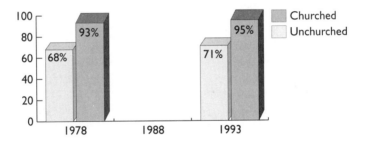

## The Church Within the Unchurched Religiosity

The local church appears to play a small role in the lives of the unchurched. This groups believes that a person can be a good Christian without attending church. The church, however, plays a large role in the development and defining of the unchurched's religiosity. The unchurched individuals who articulated their faith incorporated the church into almost every one of their religious journeys and faith stories. This incorporation does not mean that the church was portrayed in a positive light, but whether the image was positive or negative, the church did appear as people explained their faith.

This discovery says much about the church and its role in American culture. It is very difficult for Americans to separate Christianity from the church. For many people, these two ideas are almost interchangeable and inseparable. Therefore, it is necessary to talk about the church and the unchurched's view of it because it impacts their faith in some way. Either negatively or positively, the church is intertwined in their faith.

## The Church as Institutional Behavior

Some unchurched perceive church attendance to be an unnecessary trapping of Christianity and their personal faith.

> *I believe in God and His existence without a doubt; however, I do not believe in organized religion. I also do not think it is necessary for one to attend a church service to practice a religious faith.*

Many of the unchurched perceive their religious faith to be between themselves and God. The need to have such a relationship affirmed by a community of faith does not exist.

> *Religion is a personal faith, not a public affair. I feel that God knows I believe in Him, and I don't need to prove the strength of my faith to the community.*

Peter Berger talks about the need for plausibility structures in our lives. Plausibility structures are those socially manufactured fabrications that give meaning to our lives. Family, government, schools, and laws are all plausibility structures. The church is an institutionalized plausibility structure that offers a tangible expression of the Christian faith. Many unchurched have done away with this tangible plausibility structure so that the church is not a required component for their religious faith to have meaning. One young man defines the distinction the unchurched have developed between the church as an institution and their religious faith. From his statement, one recognizes that a bifurcation has occurred so that the unchurched person's personal faith becomes totally disconnected from institutionalized religion. He says,

> *I see a distinct difference between religion and spirituality, religion being an attempt of man to reach God in worship, construction of churches, etc. Spirituality for me is the personal relationship I have with Jesus. I see the two as distinctly different. Church organization is man-made and subject to fallibility; spirituality is not. For me, the church is fallible; therefore, I do not attend.*

## The Church as a Hindrance

Some of the unchurched view the church not as unnecessary, but actually as a hindrance to their religious faith. Sam H. says, "I don't feel that the church I would normally attend allows me to pursue my faith in my own way or at my own pace." Much of the hindrance is attributed to the ministers of the local congregation. Some respondents remember being scared because of the religious guilt imposed by the clergy. The following two quotes reflect the frustration of having their faith withered by professional clergy.

> *I believe in a personal God. I used to attend church, but I don't anymore. I believe God is loving and caring, not punishing. I believe you can share a message through your actions more than through preaching and condemning.*

> *I believe that religious denominations suppress the idea of Christianity and that church leaders (priests, deacons, rabbis) put forth personal opinion that persuades followers to believe as the speaker in the church would. We are all equal in the eyes of the Lord, and being a "member" of a church or denomination doesn't make us better or worse. God will accept us all as long as we make the most of what we have.*

Because of this intimidation or "brainwashing" '(as another unchurched person called it), some have reacted against Christian beliefs and developed religious beliefs and viewpoints that would not be considered orthodox Christianity. Some beliefs are clearly humanistic, while others do not correspond to current institutional beliefs. Other unchurched persons trade the church's religiosity for other world, Eastern, or New Age forms of faith or even secular forms of "religiousness" such as family and work.

Many unchurched persons are unsure of their beliefs and find that the church cannot answer their questions. They are actually searching for meaning and answers to life's questions, but they believe the church does not have those answers. The quotes below are provided as examples of these different versions of religiosity. Each of them expresses a way in which the unchurched have tried to discover and maintain their faith.

## Movement away from Traditional Christianity

*I have not found any church that meets my religious needs. My beliefs are very different from those found in most churches.*

## Institutions Substituting for the Church

*I'm a recovering alcoholic who was brought up Catholic. But since I've been sober (18 months), I've gotten a very good understanding of my higher power, which is God, but I'm not ready to start going back to a place of worship yet. That doesn't mean I'm against church, but that it is o.k. with my God that I have a very spiritual program through Alcoholics Anonymous and I work on it one day at a time.*

## Personal Spirit as Source of Meaning

*My own life is all I have to worship, by making strives for personal advancement and harmony. I'm part of the ever-growing and expanding universe. Therefore, I expand and grow with it, or I'm not reaching my potential in life. God is a point of strength for some; I gather strength through my daily trials and tribulations of life.*

## Sense of Uncertainty about Faith

*At this point in time I am unsure about God, and I have many other questions about life, but I have attended on occasion.*

## The Church as the Right Place

"Place" is very important to people. People need a "place" in which to ground themselves. Ask any minister who has ever tried to move a church member from "their seat" in a pew. We live in a world where most people are not grounded, however. People are not grounded for many reasons. Mobility is one, not so much geographic mobility as transportation mobility. Urbanized people have no problem driving 30 minutes to an hour to get somewhere.

When my parents would visit me and my wife in Louisville, Kentucky, while I was attending seminary, my father would complain every time about having to drive 30 minutes to go eat. I never thought about it, but many of our favorite restaurants were 20 minutes away from where we lived. When I moved to Clinton, South Carolina, I began to understand. At first my wife and I would hop in the car and drive 35 minutes to Greenville, South Carolina, to shop or see a movie. As time passed, we started moaning about having to drive to Wal-Mart, which is only 8 miles away. The automobile and people's willingness to ride have loosened many people's connection to the local vicinity. Connections with activities, events, and people can be found within a 30-mile radius.

The second reason people are not grounded is the shifting nature of community. People can live on a street and never know their neighbors. Relational networking is no longer dependent on proximity. In fact, relationships have nothing to do with proximity anymore. Relationship networks now develop along social lines: work, common recreational activities, common interests. These lines of networking, however, do not provide an adequate foundation for grounding either due to a lack of adequate time, physical proximity, or bonding values. Because of the loss of grounding, people are looking for the right place—a place that will give them a sense of community, a strong value-based foundation, and a firm grounding in a turbulent world.

The unchurched have had to wrestle with whether or not a church is the right place for their religious faith. This struggle bifurcates into two main categories. The first category is a group of unchurched who express a nebulous reason why they have not found the appropriate church for their lives. This response can be summed up in the statement of a middle-aged male, Arthur N.

*I haven't found a church that is right for me.*

Not finding the right church stems from several factors: personal lifestyle, theology, church's worship or ministry style, having no family or friends in a church, "getting back into the habit." One young female, Stephanie C., writes,

> *I used to go to a Lutheran school, and my family and I went to church every Sunday. For some reason though, when we moved to Louisville, we couldn't find a church we really liked. So we basically quit going, and that was ten years ago. However, that doesn't mean we quit believing.*

The other reason the religious institutions have ceased to be the "right place" for the unchurched is that such churches no longer provide meaning or motivation for many persons. Some bluntly state that the church is boring. "Why should I get up and go to church to be put to sleep by a preacher when I can sleep fine at home." Many nonchurchgoers, however, attribute their nonattendance to the church's inability to provide meaning for their lives. One female writes,

*I don't get anything from it. Also, I feel like every time you turn around, the church asks for money from you. I went to a Catholic grade school and high school, and yet I haven't gone to church on a weekly basis since the sixth grade. Now that I'm twenty, I only go to church on Christmas and Easter. I have many questions, but don't feel they could be answered at church.*

The unchurched have not lost their need for meaning and ultimate significance. They still have questions and struggle with the answers. Many, however, just no longer look to the church for the answers.

## Disillusionment with the Church

Woven into the private religious faith of many unchurched runs a more disturbing reason for affirming such religious expression. Religion and spirituality must be a private matter for the unchurched because they have become disillusioned with the church. This disillusionment manifests itself in three forms the church has created: religious defacement, history of social evils, and personal exclusion.

**Religious Defacement.** Many of the unchurched accuse the religious institutions of religious defacement. These institutions have turned from their true spiritual purpose to a worldly mindset of money and power. One individual vehemently affirms this shifting of purpose.

*I believe that churches, etc. prostitute religion. Organized religion is a big marketing scam. Religion A thinks that Religion B is wrong and going to hell.*

This person expresses the feelings of many unchurched. Such concern with organizational, financial, and worldly matters emerged in the research of Gallup's studies and Hoge's study of the dropout Catholics as well.[3] All organizations must be concerned with maintenance. Daniel Katz and Robert Khan say that the basic principle of any organization "is the preservation of the character of the system."[4] Churches, like any organization, must be concerned about their preservation and survival. Yet churches must be aware that overemphasis of such maintenance concern is a detriment to their witness.

**History of Social Evils.** Another form of disillusionment with organized religion manifests itself in a recounting of the social evils instigated by the church. Such knowledge of the history of the church is surprising and implies that some unchurched persons have experience in a religious setting. It is quite surprising to have unchurched persons recount the turbulent history of an institution with which they do not identify. An older female writes,

> *I believe that organized religion is an evil thing. It has been responsible (the Christian/Catholic religion mostly) for wars and oppression, out-of-control birth rates, hatred, intolerance, and many other social ills . . . too much immorality in the name of superiority: repressing other religions, the Crusades, American slavery, repression, killing of Native Americans, and Jim and Tammy Baker and Pat Robertson.*

Again, the church of the past haunts the church of the present. The church has never possessed a Teflon coating. Negative things have always stuck to it. And because of its divine mission and message of concern and caring, then its transgressions seem much more ominous.

**Personal Exclusion.** The final form of disillusionment with organized religion relates to the exclusionary actions of some churches. The unchurched comment that the church excludes based on race, economic status, and morality. One angry young woman tells of her mother's experience with the exclusionary practices of organized religion. She writes,

> *My mother was kicked out of the Catholic religion for marrying a divorced man. Since then, we have stayed away from the church, much to my mother's dismay. Time is too precious to waste a Sunday morning reviewing a book written thousands of years ago. And that's all it is, a book. Just because she married a divorced man, does that mean she lost her faith? I don't think so. That's why I don't believe in church. Who gives them the right to judge?*

This exclusionary practice should not be associated with church discipline. Churches have the scriptural right to instruct and correct their members in the areas of morality and appropriate behaviors. Most stories of exclusionary practices do not correspond to the carrying out of church discipline but to practices motivated by prejudice, hatred, and jealousy.

### The Most Popular Answer: Time

The most popular reason for not attending church, thus effecting a need for a private religious faith, is quite obvious. Most nonchurchgoers admit that they do not have the time for the church. It is not because they see the church as the cause of social evils. Most have not had a bad experience with the church that has left them bitter. They still see the church as a positive force where questions of life can be answered, but they just do not have the time to attend.

Time has become a rare and precious commodity in American society. More and more opportunities and responsibilities place demands and restrictions on our time. Many of these opportunities and responsibilities are good and healthy for our lives; some are not. But whether they are good or bad, they are there. We race around our daily lives as if time is running out. Since time runs out like money does, Americans are greedy with their time. Like money, we spend our time in the same way. What we purchase with our time must have value. It must give us a good return on our investment and be fulfilling to our lives or meet a need. My friends, it is as simple as that. *People will attend church (spend their time) if what they receive from church is fulfilling to them or meets a need.* Theology, denomination preference, and proximity are all secondary considerations for most of the unchurched.

**Work.** Work has become the main consumer of people's time. Most nonchurchgoers do not have time for the church because they work. Their work occurs on Sundays, and they cannot get off, or else they work late Saturday and sleep in on Sunday. In her intriguing yet disturbing book, *The Overworked American*, Juliet Schor discovers that the average American works one month more a year than did his or her predecessor twenty years earlier. In the days of increasing technology, how can this be? Technology does not save people time; it just creates the ability to do more and more with the time one has, which then expands to consume more time. Other reasons include the employer's desire to get more production out of less people, Americans' addiction with consumption, and thus the willingness to trade their time for money. Schor reported that a third of the population in 1995 believed that they were rushed to do things in their daily lives—a 25% increase from 1965.

Work also consumes much of people's lives because Americans have not only chosen to work overtime, but most find themselves in dual, triple, and even quadruple income families. Add to this, money does not buy as much as it used to. Schor quotes a twenty-eight-year-old factory worker who says, "Either I can spend time with my family or support them—not both." What little time is left over after work and family (if any), the church gets to compete for against other social opportunities such as television, sporting events, leisure, and household chores.

**Other Opportunities.** Many persons are too busy with other activities to include organized religion in their schedules. When they are not working, they are spending their leisure time. Social psychologists tell us that leisure is a primary component in overall quality of life. Leisure is not just relaxing in the chair watching TV. Leisure incorporates a wide range of activities. Two key ingredients of leisure that attribute to a high quality of life are active recreation and competence. Seppo Iso-Ahola writes,

> Leisure satisfaction cannot be improved merely by increasing the number and variety of services available. It is the individual who, either by himself or with the help of others, has to make some of the available services personally meaningful activities before they can contribute to personal leisure satisfaction.[5]

In order for a leisure activity to be meaningful, a person must achieve competence in that activity. In light of decreasing knowledge of basic Christianity and the inability of people to articulate their faith, the church is not providing the proper training to ensure competence in such matters, which is necessary if the church is to remain a viable choice among leisure time activities.

Other opportunities include education and family. Many adults have returned to school. The number of adult students in the United States has increased dramatically over the past decade. Employers are sending their workers back to school to improve or sharpen their old skills and to learn new ones. Add to this the need for further education or job training so one can get a promotion or raise, advance their own skills, or just maintain their current position as jobs change due to increasing technology. The emphasis on family is on the upswing in our nation. This is a positive trend, but it does affect the amount of time people have. After recounting all the demands on her life, one single mom says, "And with all this, I'm expected to go to church?"

Time or the lack of it plays an integral part of the unchurched's view of the church and thus affects their perception of their own religious faith. It is very easy for them to rationalize away the need for active participation in the local church as an integral part of their religious faith since their current time schedule does not allow for it. Interestingly, the majority of unchurched who stated that the lack of time was their reason for not attending church said that they planned to go back to church at some time. Lack of hours in a day is not the real factor here. The real factor is how the unchurched choose to spend those hours. Churches must begin to affect how these persons spend their time by providing programming, ministry, worship, and fellowship that is meaningful and fulfilling. When churches begin to offer such meaning and fulfillment, then time will become less of a factor.

## The Religiosity of the Unchurched

Most nonchurchgoers are pro-religious, feel the need for meaning in their lives, and approve of prayer and private religious development. Combine that evidence with the conclusions of other researchers who suggest that the unchurched may have abandoned the church but not faith. The result is an unchurched religiosity based on the Christian faith but supplemented by the inclusion of values and meaning from other sources plus the emergence of the idea that faith is a private matter and has no need for institutional grounding. Robert Bellah believes that modern society has moved from a dual-plex system of meaning to a multiplex system of meaning. Therefore, the meaning systems of the unchurched include many aspects of traditional Christianity combined with other elements drawn from other nontraditional religious systems of meaning. In a society of choice, eclecticism has been incorporated into the nature of religious faith for many of the unchurched.

### A Private Affair

Obviously, the preferred nature of religiosity for the unchurched is a private one. This attribute of the unchurched religiosity removes it from the public sphere of ritual practice and communal inspection to the private sphere of personal belief. Luckmann and Bellah speak of differentiation of society that bifurcates the society into the public and private sphere. Bellah writes,

> Religion is displaced from its role as guardian of the public world-view that gives human life its coherence. Religion is now regulated to the purely private sphere.[6]

Not only is the unchurched religiosity a private affair, it appears to hold no special status among its privatized counterparts. Time, work, and family all enter into decisions about religious faith. Differentiation not only removes religion from its public existence; it also removes its unequivocal status within the private sphere. The unchurched religiosity becomes "merely one variety of possible private options."[7]

## An Internal Focus

Not only is the unchurched religiosity a private matter, it is an internal one as well. Another person states,

> *Besides, my beliefs are really my own. I can observe my faith in my own way.*

The religiosity of the unchurched has replaced the ritual of attending church with a more private, internal religious behavior: prayer.

> *I believe in God, but I don't believe in the church because it deals too much with materialism and using God to get what they need. I believe that private prayer is just as important and useful to me.*

This internalization of the unchurched's religiosity accounts for their unwillingness to express their faith publicly or allow it to influence their public lives. The inward focus even hinders their expression of their faith in the private arena. They either do not want to discuss their faith, or they lack the ability to discuss it. If such a trend continues, there will be many unchurched persons who know so little about Christianity that even their faith will disappear.

## Cognition over Behavior

Another peculiar aspect of the unchurched religiosity is its emphasis on cognition and self-understanding and its de-emphasis on behavior. The unchurched believe themselves to be religious individuals. Many are even unsatisfied with the state of their religious faith. They feel the need for faith in God and understanding of ultimate matters. Yet this cognition does not translate into an equal emphasis on private religious behavior. Such a de-emphasis on behavior could be the result of the changing nature of unchurched religiosity. Scripture reading may no longer be the religious symbolism that expresses religious commitment and faith, whereas prayer is. The lack of time is another reason for the de-emphasis on religious behavior. This reason is quite evident for me every time I remind myself that I need to exercise.

## Religious Symbolism

An interesting development in the unchurched religiosity is the way in which the unchurched "package" their faith. People "package" their faith in religious symbolism. Religious symbolism represents the way in which the supernatural transcendence of God; the concepts of salvation, redemption, and holy mystery; and the means for mediating between the mundane and the sacred worlds are wrapped in something tangible so human beings can relate to it. The concepts, ideas, and realities do not change; only the religious symbolism in which they are wrapped changes.

In the case of the unchurched, they appear to be creating their own personal, private religious symbolism. They believe that the church cannot offer meaning for their lives, when actually the church is not offering the religious symbolism that appeals or speaks to the unchurched. The meaning the unchurched are looking for is the knowledge and salvation of Jesus Christ. It is still present, true, and valid, but the symbolism in which the church packages the message does not connect. We need to be reminded, as Bellah suggests, that "our socially constructed conception of how things really are is seriously out of date."[8] An unchurched religiosity may diverge from the traditional Christian symbolism; yet, according to many of their responses, the symbolism, however packaged, points to the same unchanging realities. Such changing religious symbolism must be addressed by churches, both theologically and ministerially.

### Strong Belief in Personal Faith

Yet amid all of this discussion of internalization of their faith, lack of religious behavior and knowledge, and the variation in the symbolism of faith, the unchurched strongly believe that they are religious people. They believe in the importance of religion in the lives of people and in their own lives. They see the need to grow spiritually and in the understanding of their faith. They are even dissatisfied with their apparent lack of religious growth. The unchurched religiosity truly is a paradox between belief and behavior.

### The Composite Picture

Many variables make up the religiosity of the unchurched in America. It is a combination of personal meaning systems, perceptions of the church, American values, and personal experience. It can be viewed as a spectrum with a multitude of variations and combinations. The composite includes internally directed faith, need for spiritual advancement, perceived problem with time, search for meaning, and the value of consumerism.

**Internally Directed Faith.** The unchurched have a personal faith normally very grounded in the Christian faith. It is private and usually expressed through prayer. It is inward-directed, and so they do not publicly express their faith. Connected to this is the lack of articulation of their faith probably because the unchurched have not struggled with what they believe. Add to this the possible lack of biblical knowledge.

**Need for Spiritual Advancement.** The unchurched recognize that they are not where they need to be spiritually. They see the need for advancement. They are hindered by time, lifestyle, and discovering fulfilling sources of meaning.

**Perceived Problem with Time.** The unchurched see time as a major problem. In many cases, people fill their time with events that bring fulfillment to their lives. They spend their time on events that offer the best return for their investment. Having no time for church is a perceived problem, but actually people have time—they just spend it on other things. Remember, however, perception is as powerful as reality.

**Search for Meaning.** All human beings search for meaning. A few are satisfied with reliance on superficial meaning systems. Most people look for deeper sources of meaning. The unchurched are searching for meaning. It is not something they do consciously everyday, but they continue to search. The modern world offers them several sources of meaning, and most unchurched persons will pick and choose from different ones to form their own systems of meaning.

**The Value of Consumerism.** The unchurched are products of their culture. The American culture has incorporated into the religiosity of the unchurched the values of consumerism and individual choice. This value of consumerism is one reason the unchurched choose from various sources of meaning; they like to have variety and choice.

## Conclusion

As one can tell, the religiosity of the unchurched is grounded in their everyday human experiences. Even their search for meaning functions in this world. They look for answers to questions and problems in their lives in the human world because they are either uncomfortable with or unfamiliar in dealing with the spiritual world. How then does an institution like the church that deals greatly with spiritual matters speak to such a religiosity? The remaining chapters address how churches need to adapt their sometime imposing spiritual "walls" to reach the unchurched where they are—in the everyday world. The church must not only be reactive to the unchurched religiosity; it must take steps in being proactive in order to shape the unchurched religiosity.

## Notes

[1]James Fowler, *Stages of Faith: The Psychology of Human Development and the Quest for Meaning* (San Francisco: Harper & Row, 1976) 14.

[2]See Charles Y. Glock, "Departures from Conventional Religion: The Nominally Religious, the Nonreligious, and the Alternatively Religious," in *The Religious Dimension: New Directions in Quantitative Research*, ed. R. Wuthnow (New York: Academic Press, 1979); Charles Y. Glack and Rodney Stark, *American Piety* (Berkeley CA: University of California Press, 1968).

[3]See George Gallup, *The Unchurched* (Princeton NJ: The Princeton Religious Research Center, 1978) and *The Unchurched: 10 Years Later* (Princeton NJ: The Princeton Religious Research Center, 1988); and Dean Hoge, *Converts, Dropouts, and Returnees: A Study of Religious Change Among Catholics* (New York: Pilgrim Press, 1981).

[4]Daniel Katz and Robert Kahn, "Organizations and the System Concept," in *Classics of Organization* Theory, ed. J. Shafritz and S. Ott (Pacific Grove CA: Brooks/Cole, 1978) 258.

[5]Seppo E. Iso-Ahola, *The Social Psychology of Leisure and Recreation* (Dubuque IO: Wm. C. Brown, Co., 1980) 384, quoted by Robert Bellah, "Discerning Old and New Imperatives in Theological Education," *Theological Education*, 19 (1982) 12.

[6]Bellah.

[7]Ibid.

[8]Robert Bellah, "Christian Faithfulness in a Pluralistic World," in *Postmodern Theology: The Church in a Pluralistic World*, ed. Frederick B. Burnham (New York: Harper & Row, 1989) 77.

# Chapter 5

# TRANSFORMING THE WALLS
## *The Unchurched Religiosity's Impact on the Church*

The Christian church in the United States finds itself functioning within a society it no longer recognizes. Robert Bellah, commenting on the modern church's societal perception, wrote, "Our socially constructed conception of how things really are is seriously out of date."[1] The walls in which we American churchgoing Christians gather every Sunday have shielded us from the changing social context outside. In fact, we have become so isolated behind these walls, we have failed to recognize that the society's perception of the "walls" has changed.

For American society, the Christian church is no longer seen as the sacred keeper of the holy power where people must come to partake. It no longer is seen as a necessary part of a person's faith. The church has allowed the world to dictate the church's new position in society and to decide the church's destiny. It is time for the church to take control of its own destiny. We have allowed the world and its shifting cultural change to regulate the church out of the people's religious faith. To correct this situation and retake control of our own destinies, local churches must start transforming their own walls so that the message of Jesus Christ and his salvation will be presented in ways that connect with the lives and the faith of the unchurched.

Transformation must occur in reaction to what we have discovered about the faith of the unchurched. Churches can no longer sit and wait for people to come to them. The church must go to the people. We must begin where they are. Paul wrote, "When I was a child, I spoke like a child, I thought like a child, I reasoned like a child; when I became an adult, I put an end to childish ways" (1 Cor 13:11). Paul was aware that we all start as children.

The unchurched are at the stage of the child. We cannot expect them to operate at a mature level, so why do most of our "entrances" to the church have prerequisites of maturity? If a local church is going to begin a transformation of itself so that the unchurched in its community find it open, responsive, and relevant to them, we must seek healing, distinguish between privatization and community, seek meaning, develop new theologies, change our image, and be aware of our language and paradigms. These steps toward transformation are discussed in reference to the different components of the religiosity of the unchurched.

Remember, we are seeking to change the "walls" of our churches so that those outside will find the church more relevant. The foundation of the church never changes. Jesus said, "I am the way, and the truth, and the life. No one comes to the Father except through me." Churches can never accommodate on this foundational tenet of our faith. Because Jesus is the truth, we seek to make our presentation of that message more relevant. Our modern society may have created social structures and philosophies that allow people to believe that multiple sources of meaning for life exist, but we Christians must always hold forth the truth that Jesus Christ is the only way. We should never be ashamed of claiming that we have found the true answer to life's questions. The foundation of our faith must never change, no matter in what landscape it finds itself. Our "walls" need to adapt, but our foundation must remain firm.

## Seek Healing

The story in Mark 2:1-6 about the paralytic man and his four friends is one of my favorite stories in the Gospels. I like it because it contains many messages most readers of the Scripture fail to recognize. I love preaching on the passage, leading the congregation down the very familiar story line of the persistence and helpfulness of the man's friends and how we should strive to help each other, and then taking a severe right turn and talking about how the church keeps people away from Jesus.

> When he returned to Capernaum after some days, it was reported that he was at home. So many gathered around that there was no longer room for them, not even in front of the door; and he was speaking the word to them. Then some people came, bringing to him a paralyzed man, carried by four of them. And when they could not bring him to Jesus because of the crowd, they removed the roof above him; and after having dug through it, they let down the mat on which the paralytic lay. When Jesus saw their faith, he said to the paralytic, "My son, your sins are forgiven." Now some of the scribes were sitting there, questioning in their hearts.

The church can be represented by the crowds surrounding the house and the scribes. Most of them were unaware that they were keeping the paralytic man away from Jesus. Others were probably quite aware. Without the persistence of his friends, the crowds would have successfully kept the paralytic man away from Jesus. Most Christians are unaware that by failing to live as witnesses to Jesus, we keep people away from Jesus. Many churches, however, are quite aware of who they choose to keep away either due to prejudice or spite.

Many nonchurchgoers are disillusioned people, scarred by the church. The church as an institution has not remained unsoiled by the evils of the world. It has been guilty of religious defacement, social injustices, and exclusionary activities. Many local churches have forged an image of saintly piety and shiny perfection and thus have alienated those who do not measure up. Because the church in general and local churches in particular have soiled histories, healing must occur. Before the church can begin ministering to the needs of the unchurched, however, it must first heal the scars it has created.

In 1995, the Southern Baptist Convention adopted a resolution apologizing to the African-American community for the convention's historical involvement in, support of, and creation over the issue of slavery. The resolution was received with mixed reviews by the African-American community and should be seen only as a first step, but the resolution was at least a step toward healing. I pray that such a resolution will be acted out in our churches.

The most common form of disillusionment with the church is, by far, personal exclusion. In my own denomination, divorce is one type of personal exclusion that has caused much hurt. The saying goes that we will forgive someone for being an axe murderer, but just don't get divorced. Though it reaches its most heated encounters when applied to the service of a deacon (for instance, many Southern Baptist churches hold to the belief that a deacon should be the husband of one wife; thus divorce would prohibit someone from being a deacon), divorce still carries a strong social stigma in many churches. A local church subtlety, and many times unknowingly, gives the impression that if someone is divorced, then they have been relegated to the rank of a second-class citizen. Most of our adult Bible study classes are for married couples, with the divorced individuals relegated to a single-again class or no class at all. Many divorced individuals do not feel comfortable in married couples classes. They may have a personal misconception about being divorced and the church's reaction to it, but many times I have to ask the church why divorced people feel uncomfortable unless they somehow have perceived that the church believes married people are better.

Healing can occur and future scarring can be avoided if local churches will begin developing a balance between conviction and compassion. Christianity is a moral religion. Sin exists in the world. The church must be convicted that certain behaviors and ideas are wrong and immoral. We should stand firm on those moral convictions and not apologize for having them, but we must balance that conviction with compassion. "We must condemn the sin and not the sinner."

It is very difficult for people to separate criticism of a behavior from personhood. Many times a person will have her self-esteem shattered when someone else criticizes something she did. The other person may have been quite adept at properly criticizing the inappropriate behavior and not the individual as a person. Still, it is difficult for us to separate our behavior from ourselves. We feel that our very being is threatened. At the same time, many of us, especially the church, cannot criticize properly. We make no distinction between the behavior and the person. They are one and the same. To avoid this form of destructive conviction, we must look to Jesus.

Jesus maintained a balance between conviction of sin and compassion for the sinner. John 8:10-11 reads,

> Jesus . . . said to her, "Woman, where are they? Has no one condemned you?" She said, "No one, sir." And Jesus said, "Neither do I condemn you. Go your way, and from now on do not sin again."

Jesus was quite frank with the woman that she had sinned and that she should cease her adulterous actions in the future, but he did not abandon the woman to the mob that called for her death. He did not condemn her; rather, he offered forgiveness. To maintain a balance between conviction and compassion, the church must learn to be convicted about the sin and show compassion to the person.

Healing and a balance between conviction and compassion can be maintained at three levels within a local church: structure, language, and personal witness.

### Structure

Structure refers to the organization of a local church, its programs, committees, by-laws, rules of membership, and so on. It is the framework in which the church operates on a day-to-day basis. Church structure must be examined for any signs of personal exclusion, religious defacement, or social injustice. Does the Bible study structure of having all adult couples classes give the impression that if you aren't married, you don't belong? Does your calendar contain too many fund-raising events or business meetings that give the impression that money and business are the church's top concern? Are there physical structures that prevent the elderly, disabled, or children from freely moving throughout the church?

> *Rule #1: A local church has every right to make rules and regulations by which it can expect its members to abide so long as those rules and regulations are based on theological convictions and not spite or prejudice (such things can be confused). It is wrong for any church to exclude persons by making them feel soiled and unclean.*

## Language

Language is too limiting to be all things to all people. It becomes quite cumbersome when one tries to address every possible circumstance. I remember a fellow seminarian who was struggling with a Mother's Day sermon. He said, "If I speak about motherhood, I will offend the single women or married women who have no children. What about the Smith family who lost a child two years ago?" I felt for my friend and understood the dilemma. Yet to try and address the complexities that exist in church bodies all at once would be cumbersome, mind-boggling, and exhaustive. My friend had the right idea but needed to spread it out over time.

> *Rule #2: We must give the appropriate amount of time to all the complexities within our churches. We must speak to senior adults, empty nesters, baby boomers, baby busters, DINKs, Generation X, builders, and so on, but we must do it over time. Churches must avoid playing the same key.*

## Personal Witness

A church's personal witness is hard to control. A local church can have an open and inclusive structure. It can be aware of its language and speak to all complexities. All of this, however, is for naught if those intentions are not seen in the personal witness of its members. If someone perceives that the members of a local church think the Scarlet A ought to make a comeback, then that church has no hope of impacting the person. Even the most subtle hint from a member that something in the person "is wrong," and the church will lose the person.

*Rule #3: If you plan to change your church structure and language, make sure your members are aware of the change and incorporate it into their personal witness.*

## Distingish Between Privatization and Community

A very familiar passage of Scripture encourages us to continue to assemble together as a community of believers in Jesus Christ. Hebrews 10:22-25 reads,

> Let us approach with a true heart in full assurance of faith, with our hearts sprinkled clean from an evil conscience and our bodies washed with pure water. Let us hold fast to the confession of our hope without wavering, for he who promised is faithful. And let us consider how to provoke one another to love and good deeds, not neglecting to meet together, as is the habit of some, but encouraging one another, and all the more as you see the day.

Normally, we churchgoers like to quote the King James Version of verse 25—"not forsaking the assembling of ourselves together"—when addressing the subject of the unchurched. But the implication of assembling together is much broader. It includes encouraging one another, stimulating each other to love and good deeds. It is not mere gathering in a single place at a certain time.

Religious privatization seems to imply the end of the religious community, mainly the church. Right? Wrong. Religious privatization only signifies a choice that now can be made but in the past was not a possibility. Any religion, however, no matter what its origins, must be practiced in community and sustained by a community. If it is not, then it is considered magic. Emile Durkheim showed that both magic and religion possess beliefs, rituals, symbols, and experiences, but only religion is practiced in a community.[2]

Not only does not religious privatization not signify the end of the religious community, it does not even signify that those who practice a privatized religion have ceased to give up on community. We do live in a very fragmented world where the lives of people are splintered into separate shards of their existence: social, economical, political, spiritual, and educational. People do not seek to hide themselves in the individual fragments of their lives. In fact, they seek and strive for community. They just seek it in a different way.

In *A Generation of Seekers*, Wade Clark Roof states that the baby boomer seekers of the world love community. They do not, however, find community in the standardized places established by their predecessors. They are looking for the qualities of community, not a place of community. The passage from Hebrews speaks not just of assembling together but also of developing a sincere heart, being sprinkled clean from evil, stimulating others to good deeds and love, and encouraging one another. Therefore, any place or group can offer them community so long as that place or group possesses the qualities of community: caring, support, accountability, commitment. Now they may find spiritual community in a place far removed from a local church. This idea is something churches have not yet discovered.

I get bent out of shape when I hear someone say, "Why should we go to them? They know where the church is"—as though the church still possesses something people will seek out. Sure, they may know where the church is; but frankly, Scarlet, the unchurched don't care. For them, the local church no longer possesses a monopoly on spiritual community. For many, a local church does not even possess a spiritual community. Their spiritual communities are not found in an established place, but in a place that possesses certain qualities.

Churches must seek to become places of spiritual community by developing the qualities of community. The number-one evangelistic tool is the personal witness of a family member or friend. Why? Because amid the network of family and friends people find the qualities of caring, support, accountability, and commitment. Direct marketing, advertising, visitation, and special events are all effective tools in reaching the unchurched. The primary tool, however, is the network of friends and family within the church membership. If those networks are not being utilized, then that church is missing a large majority of its evangelistic potential.

## Seek Meaning

In 1990, I read a book that would forever change my perspective on church work and dealing with people in the modern world. The book was written by Harvard sociologist Daniel Yankelovich and focused on his work concerning the cultural ethics within generations.[3] In the book, Yankelovich talks about the rise of a new cultural ethic—the ethic of self-fulfillment. The ethic of the older generation of Americans is an ethic of self-denial. The people who operated under this ethic felt the need to deny themselves for their families, their work, and their religion. They understood life as duty and responsibility to someone or something else.

Out of this self-denial ethic grew a great amount of loyalty. Such loyalty to family was a reason for low divorce rates. A man stayed with one company for his entire career. Church attendance was the way in which people showed their loyalty to their God.

With the coming of the baby boomers, a new ethic began to form: the ethic of self-fulfillment. This ethic does not sound as noble as the old ethic and can be construed as selfishness on the part of the baby boom and subsequent generations. It has at the root of it essence the idea that a person has a duty not to family, work, or church, but to him/herself. Yankelovich states that this ethic of self-fulfillment is based on the foundational idea that life is intrinsically valuable and, therefore, should be enjoyed. Yankelovich recognizes that such a cultural ethic could lead to a depraved, selfish society, but he believes that it does not have to do so.

Self-fulfillment can be found in commitment to family and work and faith. The surge in the importance of family can be attributed to this ethic of self-fulfillment. People find their families to be fulfilling to their lives. People choose their careers and particular jobs because they are fulfilling. The high rate of job changes is also related to the ethic of self-fulfillment as people struggle to find the job that not only provides for their financial needs but is fulfilling to them.

In their book, *The New Individualists: The Generation after the Organizational Man*, Paul Leinberger and Bruce Tucker parallel Yankelovich's theory in their study of commitment to corporations. The old generation workers—the generation of the organizational man—stayed with a company for their entire careers. The company rewarded the individuals with job security, and the individuals in return gave their undying loyalty and commitment to the company. The new generation of workers (and companies) is not so committed. Leinberger and Tucker state that the new breed of workers uses the company, and when the work is no longer fulfilling the employees leave.

So what about the church? The traditions, structures, and environments in the large majority of churches today were created by the generation that held to the ethic of self-denial. Churches have lost ground with the generation that holds to the ethic of self-fulfillment for this very reason. When we hear the words, "the church no longer offers any meaning to me," we hear the cry of the ethic of self-fulfillment. This does not mean that the church's message has suddenly become invalid. What has become invalid is the way the message is packaged. Local churches must begin to package the message so that it is appealing to a new cultural ethic.

I teach a singles Sunday School class of baby boomers and busters. A particular Bible study was on Matthew 16:24.

> If any want to become my followers, let them deny themselves and take up their cross and follow me. For those who want to save their life will lose it, and those who lose their life for my sake will find it. For what will it profit them if they gain the whole world but forfeit their life? Or what will they give in return for their life?

I agonized over teaching such a lesson to a room full of people who adhered to an ethic of self-fulfillment. I further questioned if the idea of a religion based on denial of self could ever be accepted by such a generation. Thank the Lord for divine insight. I began thinking about myself. I am in this same generation. Why do I adhere to this self-denying religion? Because in the denying of myself to the lordship of Jesus Christ I gain the fulfillment of my life. The message is not and never will be invalid. We must learn, however, to package it in a new way.

## Develop New Theological Approaches

Jesus said in Matthew 5:17, "Do not think that I have come to abolish the law or the prophets; I have come not to abolish but to fulfill." Though the Pharisees and other religious leaders saw Jesus as a threat to their theologies, Jesus came not to destroy their theologies but to transform them so they would point to God's ultimate revelation: Jesus. One way in which Jesus transformed the theologies of the day was to present his revelation of God and himself in very common terms. With the use of parables and teachings that incorporated the agrarian culture of his time, Jesus presented his message of salvation to the lowly and common as well as to the high and lofty.

Do our theological approaches need to change as society changes? The answer to such a question depends on one's perspective of what a theology is. One can view theology as the unchanging reality of the sacred cosmos, those basic tenets of belief in God, Jesus, and salvation. Obviously such a view of theology does not change in reaction to fluctuating societal trends. One can also view theology as the religious symbolism in which human beings have tangibly clothed their understanding of the divine. Religious symbolism is nothing more than the ways we express our understanding of God. With this view, one can say that theologies need to change in relation to societal changes. I believe we can hold to both views. We obviously have doctrines of faith and belief that cannot nor should not be changed in light of changing social realities. However, many traditions and ceremonies by which we clothe those unchangeable beliefs should change in light of changing social realities.

This second view of theology is the perspective I choose for this discussion. If theology is a set of religious symbols and mechanisms that explain our understanding of the divine, then our theological approaches or religious symbols and mechanisms must change in order to be relevant to the present society. For example, hymns are religious mechanisms by which we express the nature of God, Jesus, the church, and salvation. Hymns convey those unchangeable truths of our faith. Do hymns need to change in light of social realities? The truths they convey should not change, but their style of music and use of language should. I realize that the idea of changing hymns could be a major battle in many churches, but we must admit that hymns are merely mechanisms through which we express our unchanging faith. Churches that are attracting the unchurched recognize this and have changed their mechanisms (hymns to praise songs) but not the message.

Such change does not insinuate that a church is becoming worldly. It does suggest that a church is attempting to change its theological approaches in order to reach the world outside its walls. Jim Waites, president of the Association of Theological Schools, recognizes the need for new theological approaches.

> Many in that generation (30–45) are not turned off by religion, just unpersuaded that the churches they know are essential to their faith. . . . The defection of the modern generation toward organized religion may well be explained by the failure of the church to speak with an articulate, contemporary theological voice.

In response to this lack of a contemporary theological voice, Waites calls for "new theologies that are responsive to the language and vernacular of today's culture."[4] These new theologies must reflect the contextual situation of North American society. Again, the development of new theological approaches does not mean abandoning the essentials of our faith, but rather changing the symbols and mechanisms we use to express them.

Much of what the unchurched believe appears to be grounded in their human existence. Therefore, an adequate theology for this population must incorporate human, everyday concerns into its theological system in a manner relevant for the unchurched's search for meaning. The search for meaning and answers to existence are important parts of

the unchurched religiosity. Twentieth-century theologians John Macquarrie and Paul Tillich can provide starting points for this theological search
for meaning and ultimate significance.[5]

Macquarrie argues for the idea of "dialectical interaction" as a viable
concept of God. Dialectical interaction pictures God and the world in a
dynamic, ever-changing interaction with each other in which God is
actively involved in everyday life. Dialectical interaction stands in oppo-
sition to classical theism at the point of the relationship of God to the
human world. Classical theism presents God as "distinctly transcendent,
separate from and over or above the world. The transcendence and
majesty of God are not sufficiently qualified by recognition of His immanence and humility."[6] Classical theism presents God as "holier than
thou," a God whose presence cannot be approached by mere human
beings. Picture Moses on Mount Sinai standing in the cleft of the rock as
he confronts God. Here is the God of classical theism. Here is a God who
is beyond and above everyday, human existence. Dialectical interaction,
on the other hand, incorporates an interaction between human beings
and the sacredness of God as seen through the life, death, and resurrection of Jesus Christ. If Moses standing in the cleft of the rock pictures
classical theism, then Jesus' ministry on earth pictures dialectical
interaction.

Macquarrie offers three dialectical characteristics that speak to religiosity and the context of the unchurched. God exists as knowability and
incomprehensibility.[7] The idea of God as incomprehensible resides in the
classical theism perspective. God is mystery; God is unfathomable.
Macquarrie suggests that the concept of dialectical interaction brings
God within the realm of human knowledge. This knowledge of God is
"mediated through images and symbols."[8] God is made known to the
world through these symbols and mechanisms. Therefore, these religious
symbols and mechanisms must be relevant to the people who encounter
them. If these symbols and images are not relevant to contemporary society nor able to convey meaning to the unchurched, then people cannot
know God. The unchurched indicate that the church no longer possesses
the symbols and images that bring the knowledge of God into their daily
lives. Remember that Paul says in Colossians 1:9-10a,

> For this reason, since the day we heard it, we have not ceased pray-
> ing for you and asking that you may be filled with the knowledge of
> God's will in all spiritual wisdom and understanding, so that you
> may lead lives worthy of the Lord.

The knowledge of God comes first. Without the knowledge of God, there is no wisdom or understanding and, therefore, no faith and application.

The second dialectical characteristics of God are transcendence and immanence. Transcendence was a primary component of classical theism. God was viewed as holy other—that which is beyond the mundane world. Classical theism held God beyond the world. Macquarrie argues that God is both beyond the world and dwelling in the world. The opposite of transcendence is immanence. Immanence portrays God as "indwelling in creation."[9] This indwelling in the world should not be mistaken as some passive pantheism in which God is nature. The indwelling is active. Many of the unchurched feel that God actively influences their lives. They look toward a personal encounter with God who meets them in their personal, private faith.

A phenomenon sweeping through the Southern Baptist Convention is "Experiencing God" by Henry Blackaby. One of Blackaby's main ideas is that God is doing something in the world, and Christians need to discover what it is and get on board. Jesus' life is the ultimate manifestation of God's immanence. In the life of Jesus as God in everyday existence, he experienced the same trials and joys and temptations we experience. Churches must begin preaching and teaching God's immanence, as seen through Jesus, as well as God's transcendence so that the unchurched can see an active, relevant God at work in our churches.

The final dialectical combination that connects with the religiosity of unchurched individuals is God as eternal and temporal. The eternal concept of God relates to the transcendence and incomprehensibility of God. The unchurched religiosity does not identify with a God who resides on the other side of life . . . in eternity. The unchurched are "this worldly" not "otherworldly." Their concerns lie in what happens in this world (temporal), not in the world to come (eternal). An unchurched religiosity is grounded in human experience and culture. The unchurched's faith combines both eternal (sacred) and temporal (common) elements into its collective whole. Macquarrie does not define temporal as something profane, ordinary, or limited. Macquarrie uses the term temporal to denote the close, everyday activity of God in the temporal lives of human beings. Such active presence in the temporal world is a necessary component for the God of unchurched persons. Macquarrie wrote,

> Many human beings who have been active in the realization of value have testified that it was not simply by their own efforts, and that their actions were invoked and sustained by the spirit of God in

their midst, inspiring them through divine grace. They have believed that God himself has been engaged in the struggle, and that he is not just an observer, untouched by it all, but an active participant.[10]

Macquarrie suggests that the idea that God is at work in the temporal world generates a vital spirituality that is grounded not only in the sacred cosmos but also in the everyday human existence.

Though Macquarrie believes that one's religious faith is grounded in both supernatural and human existence, the initiation of revelation comes from the transcendent level and not the human level. Jesus is God's ultimate revelation. The revelation of Jesus Christ as Savior and Lord is a gift given to human beings in their encounters with God. How one reacts to the revelation resides in the human response to God's initiative, but Macquarrie clearly indicates that the initiation is outside the human reality. He wrote,

> We do not bring into the light or strip away what is concealing it, as we do in our researches into matters within the world, but rather that which is known comes into the light, or, better still, provides the light by which it is known and by which we in turn know ourselves.[11]

A new theological approach must contain human, temporal elements, but those human components can never surpass the transcendence and revelation of God in Christ Jesus.

Paul Tillich speaks of the search for faith as a search for one's ultimate concern. Tillich believes that ultimate concern contains a dual process. He wrote, "It is not only the unconditional demand made by that which is one's ultimate concern; it is also the promise of ultimate fulfillment."[12] The idea of fulfillment has become a personal value in the American context. The unchurched search for meaning in order to be fulfilled for "every human being . . . exists in the power of an ultimate concern, whether or not he is fully conscious of it, whether or not he admits it to himself and to others."[13] Consciously or unconsciously, we all seek to be fulfilled. Ultimate concern is that place in our lives that only God in Christ Jesus can fill.

A central component of the unchurched religiosity appears to be this search for ultimate concerns, concerns that are grounded in both divine and human reality. Thomas Luckmann claims that the privatization of religion has created a state in which individuals draw their answers to ultimate concerns no longer solely from a supernatural, eternal realm but from everyday human existence as well. Tillich would agree with Luckmann. He claims,

> There is no reality, thing, or event which cannot become a bearer of the mystery of being and enter into a revelatory correlation. . . . This is the reason why about every type of reality has become a medium of revelation somewhere.[14]

God and Christ in the modern world are no longer confined to the narrow walls of the church. To say that they are is institutional arrogance. Macquarrie and Tillich claim that the reason for the departure of the unchurched from traditional Christianity to acceptance of other systems of meaning is that churches have not been able to adjust their theological approaches to adequately express the dynamic involvement of God in the world in order to address the ultimate concerns of people today.

The church finds itself unable to synchronize its powerful message of Jesus with the modern world because it will not allow its theological approaches to adapt to the modern context. The sacred theological truths retain their power; the symbols in which the church wraps those are outdated and inadequate to speak to and reach the unchurched. Local churches must develop the symbols and mechanisms that can speak to the unchurched of their communities. Such symbols and mechanisms are: justice, community service, fuflfillment, acceptance, forgiveness, celebrative worship, and relevant programming. Unfortunately, churches have found it difficult to hold forth such symbols and mechanisms. Therefore, the unchurched have begun to search for those sacred truths in other places, and in doing so develop their personal, private theologies.

In order to recapture the relevance of its theological approaches, churches need only look to the author and founder of our faith for the proper combination of theological synthesis—Jesus Christ. Jesus is the incorporation of divine and human. Tillich wrote,

> All reports and interpretations of the New Testament concerning Jesus as the Christ possess two outstanding characteristics: his maintenance of unity with God and his sacrifice of everything he could have gained for himself from this unity.[15]

Jesus provides the example of how the church must adapt its theology to the modern context. In Jesus there resides the pattern of maintaining the balance between divinity and humanity, where meaning of existence arises from both the sacred and human sources. Jesus worked out his theology in everyday, common places and events and made his theology relevant by the use of human symbols. At the same time, the message he proclaimed through these common, contemporary symbols and mechanisms pointed to another reality that lay outside the human existence. It led toward God. New theological approaches that speak to the modern context must provide a relevant explanation of existence, life, and redemption (the things human beings label as ultimate concerns). This relevant explanation must emerge from common, contemporary symbols that have their grounding in modern, human existence and the divine transcendence of God. In any case, all theological approaches must bear witness to the true revelation of God in Jesus Christ.

## Change Our Image

The Pharisees are the bad guys of the New Testament. They are normally portrayed as trying to entrap Jesus in order to discredit him or provide a reason to arrest him. The Pharisees were the religious teachers of their day and had separated themselves from the common person. To describe the gap that existed between the Pharisees and the common man, Jesus told a parable about a Pharisee and a tax collector.

> Two men went up to the temple to pray, one a Pharisee and the other a tax collector. The Pharisee, standing by himself, was praying thus, "God, I thank you that I am not like other people: thieves, rogues, adulterers, or even like this tax collector. I fast twice a week; I give a tenth of all my income." But the tax collector, standing far off, would not even look up to heaven, but was beating his breast and saying, "God, be merciful to me, a sinner!" I tell you, this man went down to his home justified rather than the other; for all who exalt themselves will be humbled, but all who humble themselves will be exalted. (Luke 18:10-14)

The publican humbly and sincerely acknowledged his shortcoming to God, while the Pharisee prided himself on not being like the tax collector.

The unchurched see churches as models of the Pharisees, a combination of perfection and hypocrisy. Either way, the reason for both labels is quite clear. Churchgoers have an image problem, and, therefore, the church has an image problem. In his insightful book, *All Consuming Images*, Stuart Ewen discusses how the advertising industry has developed within the American consumer a hunger for style and image. Americans thrive on projecting a certain image that highlights the positive characteristic of their culture. A popular series of commercials for the soft drink

Sprite blares, "Image is nothing; thirst is everything." The commercials, however, sure use a number of well-known sports images to promote their product. Sprite really knows that "image is everything."

Churches have an image problem. The problem is, most churchgoers are seen as people who are associated with a place where high moral standards, loving attitudes, and caring spirits abound. Churchgoers and the church have latched on to such images and perpetuated them to such an extent that many church members believe they are pious saints. Then when they don't act like saints, the rest of the world labels them hypocrites. Is the church a group of highly moralistic, loving, and caring spirits? It is time for the church and churchgoers to take a serious look at the image the church and its members have created.

## Image Myths

The church is not a center of godliness, though we are called to be. The church is not a gathering of perfect, pious people; all have sinned. The church is not a fraternity with secret handshakes and code words. So what kind of image must the church project? We must recognize that we as the church combine both the human and divine into our institution. No other social institution in the world has the arduous task of combining human elements with divine elements. The divine elements have constructed a divine mission. The church is called to:

> *Tell*—Evangelism is a primary function of the church. The church must be out in the world spreading the good news of Jesus Christ and his saving grace.

> *Heal*—The church is a healing place. The world is a dangerous place, mentally, emotionally, spiritually, as well as physically. The church is called to care for those who become scarred by the world.

> *Tend*—The church grows its members spiritually. The church is called to make disciples as Jesus molded his disciples. Churches must care for their flocks as Jesus cares for his flock, the entire church.

> *Defend*—The church is called to defend the moral and spiritual teachings of Jesus.

The church's divine mission is sustained by the power of Jesus Christ, and thus the church possesses a unique component that separates it from other institutions.

The divine mission of the church is only a part of who the church really is. The other side of the church is the human side. The church is a human institution. It was constructed by human beings as a way of preserving and celebrating the transcendent nature of their faith. Because it was humanly constructed and is populated by human beings, the church is inundated with human frailties. Unfortunately, these human frailties should not or, more than likely, cannot happen in church.

When I was a youth minister at a church in Louisville, Kentucky, a mother of one of my youth members stopped attending church. When I asked her why she was not attending, she told me that someone in the church had criticized the decorations she had made for the youth lock-in. When I asked her if she had trouble with criticism at work or at home, she said no. I pushed her about why this had disturbed her so. She replied, "Because you are not supposed to do that at church."

We have created an image that has not only been adopted by those outside the church but also by those inside the church, an image that when people pass through the doors of the church they are suddenly transformed into sinless, loving creatures. The church is made up of human beings who are prone to sin. The doors of the church do not act as a filtering system that eliminates all the sin particles from every person who passes through. Human mistakes happen at church. Our sinful sides show themselves at church. Individuals who walk through the doors of the church are not suddenly transformed into morally superior people.

For too long, the church has highlighted its divine image over its human image. The church has been seen as a divine place where pious people gather. We have tried to downplay the latter image of the church with human weaknesses. Yet this de-emphasis has created our image problem. The image of the church among the unchurched is that of divine calling and moral superiority.

An interview with Jimmy Johnson when he coached the Dallas Cowboys showed a clip of him addressing the team. Johnson was seen screaming, "If you are going to talk the talk, then you better walk the walk." The Cowboys and Johnson talked the talk from the day Jimmy Johnson arrived; but their first two seasons were miserable. The team and, especially, Johnson were seen as jokes. They kept talking the talk. And then they began to walk the walk and ultimately became Super Bowl champions twice. They were no longer seen as jokes because they were doing what they said they were capable of doing. How telling Johnson's line is for the church. We have for so long projected an image of divine calling and moral superiority. We have, however, failed to walk the walk. For that reason, many people see the church as a joke.

## Image Makeover

The church needs an image makeover. We need a synthesis of the divine calling and the human institution. The church must project a parallel image, an image in which the divine mission of the church is managed and dispensed by ordinary human beings. We must lose the image of Christians as perfect, godly people and rather see them as people who try to be godly people. Even though we desperately want to be and should strive to be godly, we are not. We are sinners. I offer three tenets of this parallel image.

(1) *Recognize the good, the bad, and the ugly.* God has created an elaborate environmental system that creates our weather. The same components of heat, cold, air, and water that create a glorious fall day or a soft spring rain also create tornadoes, droughts, and floods. The church has a similar system. The human components that show the love and compassion of God can also succumb to devilish temptation. Christians must rid ourselves of the image that only the good in people show up at church.

(2) *Be honest with the world.* The image of the church as a gathering of perfect people must end. Christians are not perfect and never will be. The church must admit to the world that we are a gathering of flawed people, people who have accepted that as part of being human and being a part of a human institution. In actuality, this is the very reason we are Christians. We have chosen to be Christians because of the acknowledgment of this flawed human nature. The church exists because of the desire to grapple with and deal with this flawed human nature through the redeeming power and salvation of Jesus Christ.

Christians receive most of our criticism and jeers of hypocrisy when we attempt to defend morality. We must again be honest with the world that we do not pretend to be a totally moral people. We believe in a high moral standard to which we hold ourselves as well as the world. We must also believe that the only way we will live up to that standard is through the forgiveness of God. We need to recognize and distribute the image that Christians have not joined ourselves to this institution called the church because we are morally superior or divinely insightful people. We are Christians for the very opposite reason; we recognize that we are not those things and only through the loving forgiveness and redeeming salvation of Jesus are we made whole.

(3) *Celebrate the shining moments.* Christians must project an image of trying. Most of Paul's writings were written in the subjunctive, which captures the idea of continuation. We are never finished being Christian, but we are always striving to be more Christian. We must celebrate those

shining moments when for a brief time we rise above who we humanly are and become that gathering of believers of whom Jesus spoke in Matthew 16:18, "On this rock I will build my church, and the gates of Hades will not prevail against it" and in John 13:35 "By this everyone will know that you are my disciples, if you have love for one another."

I was a youth worker one summer while attending Wake Forest University. At the end of the summer we conducted a junior high camp. One evening after our pastor had spoken about the power of prayer, he and I were in the bunkhouse with our group of seventh and eighth grade boys. We started a sentence prayer time. At the end of an hour and to the amazement of the pastor and myself, these twelve- and thirteen-year-old boys were praying powerful prayers for their families and friends. They were praying together, arm in arm. It truly was a shining moment.

\*\*\*

The church is a combination of the divine and the human just as Jesus was during his earthly ministry. We should not be Gnostic churches, dispersing the idea that the church is only divine. We live in both worlds. We must project the parallel image of divine call and human institution to those outside the walls.

## Be Aware of Language and Paradigms

For if I pray in a tongue, my spirit prays but my mind is unproductive. What should I do then? I will pray with the spirit, but I wil pray with the mind also; I will sing praise with the spirit, but I will sing praise with the mind also. Otherwise, if you say a blessing with the spirit, how can anyone in the position of an outsider say the "Amen" to your thanksgiving, since the outsider does not know what you are saying? For you may give thanks well enough, but the other person is not built up. I thank God that I speak in tongues more than all of you; nevertheless, in church I would rather speak five words with my mind, in order to instruct others also, than ten thousand words in a tongue. (1 Cor 14:14-19)

Paul recognized that many people within the community would not have the level of understanding needed to interpret the speaking in tongues and, therefore, would not be able to participate in the Christian gathering. Paul concluded that if the gift of speaking in tongues excluded people from the community of faith, then it should not be practiced. The idea of "with the spirit" can be associated with the church's otherworldly paradigm and the idea of "with the mind" can refer to a worldly paradigm. Paul said that if people would be edified, he would rather speak a limited amount in the worldly way than speak a tremendous amount in the otherworldly way. Many churches are speaking in "tongues" or paradigms that most unchurched people are unable to understand.

If we are going to be serious about reaching the unchurched, we must begin where they are. To avoid turning them off with our churchy language and other paradigms, we must refocus some of our ministry programs and many of our introductory programs to the lowest denominator. By ministry programs, I mean Bible study, discipleship training, age-focused ministries, and so on. By introductory programs, I mean visitation, worship, new member training, outreach, and evangelism. By the lowest common denominator, I mean removing our established paradigms for doing church. I mean speaking "with the mind" rather than "with the spirit." Behaviors and terms that are so common to us within our church surroundings are foreign to the unchurched. We must start at the very beginning and bring the unchurched along with us.

At workshops I ask pastors and other staff ministers, "How do you drive a car?" Most start off by telling how to press the accelerator and brake, how to turn the steering wheel, where to look to maneuver. They are quite correct, but they are assuming a lot. To start at the beginning, I need to be told to pick up the keys, go to the door, stick a certain key in the little slot in the door, open the door, sit in the seat behind the wheel, put a certain key into another little slot (the ignition), and turn it.

We assume a lot at church: where things are; when events occur; which family members go to what event; what the dress code is at each event; who Paul and Peter are; what a Leviticus is; what "thee" and "thou" mean; what "saved," "redeemed," and "justification" mean. We also assume that everyone who enters our church doors can maneuver between the natural and supernatural worlds. The unchurched are not used to operating in the supernatural realm. To be asked to do so makes them uncomfortable and anxious. It places them in a state of losing control of their surroundings. Such a state is not a positive experience, and people will not continue under such conditions.

Classic psychological studies in perceived control show that when you remove people's perceived control, they ultimately will give up. It is a psychological concept called "learned helplessness." It was first discovered in experiments with dogs. The dogs were placed in a cage with no way out. Every so often, an escape route was open. Of course, the dogs tried to get out. But as soon as the dogs were almost at the escape route, it closed and the dogs were trapped again. This procedure was repeated, and ultimately the dogs laid down and did nothing—even when the escape route was left open for an extended period. The dogs were even called to in order to get them to go through the escape route. They did not budge. They had learned helplessness. They had learned that nothing they did mattered. They had lost control over their situation, and so they did nothing to affect it.

The experiment was conducted on people in a different manner. They were placed in a room that received a random blast of annoying noise. To get out of the room, they had to complete a puzzle. The puzzle, however, was unsolvable. At first the subjects tried and tried to complete the puzzle and get out of the room with the annoying sound. After a while, however, they stopped trying. The researchers encouraged them to continue. The researchers turned the noise louder and made it more frequent. The subjects continued to do nothing. They had learned helplessness. They perceived that they had lost control, and, therefore, nothing they did would affect their situation.

When the unchurched enter a local church and encounter strange paradigms of behavior and language that cause them to lose control of their surroundings, most will choose to give up on the church rather than try and gain hold of the strange paradigms. We must create mechanisms that lower this perceived loss of control.

Seeker services are the latest attempt among churches to lower this perceived loss of control feelings. Seeker services strip away all the traditions and churchly atmosphere and trappings and operate in a more "everyday" mentality. The success of many of the seeker-style churches is largely due to the creation of a paradigm with which the unchurched are somewhat familiar.

Jim White, a friend of mine from seminary days, is pastor of the Mecklinburg Community Church. The church is geared to introducing the unchurched to Jesus through the seeker-style method. The church meets in a school and has a live band for worship. Jim preaches in a short sleeve shirt and tie. He wants the worship environment to be more like a seminar than a typical church service. When the Mecklinburg Community Church builds a campus facility of its own, Jim wants it to look like an office complex and not a traditional brick church. Seeker services are more like attending a business seminar than a church. Why? Most unchurched persons are comfortable in such a setting and, therefore, do not lose their sense of control over their surroundings.

Obviously, not all churches can sponsor seeker-style services. So what are some things a more traditional church can do?

•Establish a Bible study taught in basic biblical knowledge.

•Offer an early service that is less formal and uses more contemporary worship methods such as drama, contemporary music, a live band, and practical and less theological sermons.

•Gear promotional literature toward the "church challenged."

•Establish a mentor program in which prospects or new members are overseen for their first few months by a knowledgeable church member. This member can meet them each Sunday, get them to where they should be, explain any unwritten behavioral rules, and so on.

## Conclusion

All of these suggestions for transforming the church are in reaction to the unchurched religiosity so the unchurched will see the church as relevant and vital to their faith. Yet churches cannot be only reactive. In fact, we must stop being reactive. For too long, churches have allowed the world to pass us by and then allowed it to set the conditions for existence. Churches must be proactive. Stephen Covey, the guru of personal motivation, says of "proactivity":

> As human beings, we are responsible for our own lives. Our behavior is a function of our decisions, not our conditions. We have the initiative and the responsibility to make things happen.[16]

Though Covey's definition is geared toward the individual person, it can easily be applied to churches. Christians have allowed culture to shape the church's existence and its position in society. Christians must begin to shape our own destinies and in turn shape our culture.

## Notes

[1]Robert Bellah, "Christian Faithfulness in a Pluralistic World," in *Postmodern Theology: The Church in a Pluralistic World*, ed. Frederick B. Burnham (New York: Harper & Row, 1989) 77.

[2]Emile Durkheim, *The Elementary Forms of Religious Life*, trans. J. Swain (New York: The Free Press, 1915) 59.

[3]Daniel Yankelovich, *New Rules: Searching for Self-Fulfillment in a World Turned Upside Down* (New York: Random House, 1981).

[4]James Waites, "A Future for Theological Education," chapel address, Southern Baptist Theological Seminary, Louisville, Kentucky, 2 September 1992.

[5]Some contemporary scholars would disagree with the choice of Macquarrie and Tillich as starting points for the development of new, contemporary theologies. These scholars, especially liberation theologians, would object to Macquarrie's and Tillich's emphasis on individual existential concerns over corporate matters. Such objections are legitimate. The new theologies must seek a balance between the ultimate concerns of the individual and the corporate concerns of the community.

[6]John Macquarrie, *In Search of Deity: An Essay in Dialectical Theism* (New York: Crossroads, 1985) 31.

[7]Ibid., 175.

[8]Ibid., 176.

[9]Ibid., 177.

[10]Ibid., 182.

[11]John Macquarrie, *Principles of Christian Theology,* 2d ed. (New York: Charles Scribner's Sons, 1977) 86.

[12]Paul Tillich, *Dynamics of Faith* (New York: Harper & Row, 1957) 2

[13]Paul Tillich, *Systematic Theology,* vol. 1 (Chicago: The University of Chicago Press, 1951) 24.

[14]Ibid., 118.

[15]Ibid., 135.

[16]Stephen R. Covey, *Seven Habits of Highly Effective People* (New York: Simon & Schuster, 1989) 71.

# Chapter 6

# MINISTERING TO THE FAITH OUTSIDE
### *The Church's Impact on the Unchurched*

The church must not only strive to increase its integrity among the unchurched population by transforming some of the walls that isolate the people inside and keep out the people outside, it must also attempt to adapt to the ever-changing patterns of social life in order to impact and shape the changing patterns of religiosity among the unchurched. The majority of these persons hold a religious faith that is private, searching, and cognitive. It is also a religiosity that must "fit" into the daily lives of these individuals. Again, I am not suggesting total accommodation to the unchurched lifestyle. Rather, I am suggesting that the church impact and change the unchurched religiosity through adapting the "packaging" of its message of Jesus Christ.

The church must contextualize the message of the gospel to the worldview of the unchurched individual so that the gospel becomes the central component of the unchurched's religiosity. In the words of Byant H. Kato, contextualization means to make "concepts or ideals relevant in a given situation."[1] Such contextualization must occur on two levels: the theological level, discussed in chapter 5, and the cultural level.

Cultural contextualization means adaptation to the current cultural setting of those social means and methods used by the local church in its evangelistic and ministry efforts. Unidimensional forms of evangelism and ministry do not address the consumer mentality of the unchurched. If this were the case, then McDonald's would serve only one kind of hamburger. Yet churches persist in offering the message of salvation and hope in Jesus Christ in limited forms. If the church is going to contextualize the saving message of Jesus Christ to the culturally sensitive person outside the church, we must take a stand, give a personal witness, begin where the unchurched are, develop a market attitude, balance ministerial servanthood and authority, care for children, and produce quality programs suited to the unchurched's schedules. These steps toward cultural adaptation are discussed in reference to the different variables within the religiosity of the unchurched.

## Take a Stand

Stephen Covey's third habit of highly effective people is putting first things first. Covey encourages people to discover the important factors in life and concentrate on them. He promotes focusing on relationships and producing results rather than focusing on time and things. My church's annual theme for the past year was "Putting First Things First—Seek first the kingdom of God, and all these things shall be added unto you." If churches are to be proactive in our society, then we must put first things first. Specifically, churches must take a stand for Jesus Christ. Churches must counter modern society's gospel of multiple sources of meaning systems with the gospel of the one and only true source of meaning.

The unchurched have written off churches, not because churches have taken a stand for Jesus, but because churches have relativized Jesus. Persons outside the church are turned off by a watered-down gospel that is wishy-washy about truth and conviction. They find no meaning in such a gospel, and so they look elsewhere. Churches must return to preaching, teaching, and living biblical truths. Christians must never be ashamed of taking a stand for Jesus and claiming that Jesus is the only way, the only truth, and the only choice for abundant and eternal life.

## Give a Personal Witness

In a recent survey on effective evangelism strategies, George Barna found that personal relationship witnessing is still the most effective means of evangelism. The reaction to this, like most social research, is "we already knew that." But we need social researchers such as George Barna to remind us of what we seem to already know but do not act upon. Yes, churches are well aware that personal witnessing is the most effective means of evangelism. It is more effective than revivals, visitation, advertising, and even television. So why do most churches choose to employ all these other methods and avoid promotion of personal witnessing?

We have made people scared of witnessing. The idea of knocking on some strange door and invading the lives of strangers is not a pretty picture to most folks. Even though door-to-door witnessing is not that bleak, many people have such a perspective. In a book entitled *Team Evangelism*, the author suggests that only 10% of all church members possess the gift of evangelism—that is, sharing their faith with people whom they do not know. This means that 90% of persons with a church relationship do not possess the abilities to share the gospel with strangers. This lack of the gift of evangelism is the reason that most churches are not utilizing their most powerful evangelistic tool.

Unfortunately, churches have also used this reason as an excuse. "We designate times for visitation. We serve meals and provide child care, but still nobody comes." Why don't people take advantage of such witnessing opportunities? The reasons are numerous: lack of time, lack of the gift of evangelism, fear of intruding on strangers, and so on. So what can be done? How can the church take advantage of personal witnessing as means to growth and evangelism? Let me offer three suggestions.

First, churches need to designate a particular group for stranger evangelism. Stranger evangelism is visiting and witnessing to those who are not part of a church member's network of family or friends. Churches should identify those church members who possess the gift of evangelism and utilize them in their stranger evangelism program. To address this need in my church, I started a group called the Gideon 20. These people either volunteered or were recruited to visit visitors and prospects. They served for one year and then were not asked to serve again for two more years. They visited only once a month, which defused the time issue. They were given prospects on Sunday and would set up a visit with the prospects sometime during the week. Deacons, elders, and other church leaders should also be utilized in stranger evangelism.

Second, churches must learn to train people in sharing their faith. I am not talking about how to recite the Roman Road or following the Evangelism Explosion program, although instruction in these programs is needed. First, recruit people who are able to share about their personal relationship with Jesus. People are not unwilling or embarrassed to share their faith, but they are fearful of not being able to properly articulate their faith and respond to possible questions. Again, I remind you of the finding that biblical knowledge is at an all-time low. The average church members have not adequately wrestled with or thought about their faith enough to develop a well-formulated presentation of it. Training people in leading an unchurched person to Christ is good, but the first step is teaching people how to understand, express, and articulate their own faith and testimony.

Third, churches must develop in their members the idea of personal relationship witnessing. Personal relationship witnessing is nothing more than lifestyle evangelism in which persons take advantage of their network of relationships in sharing their faith and leading others toward a relationship with Jesus Christ. This form of witnessing does not require the gift of evangelism since one is working within previously established relationships. It allows persons to take their time in deciding when to share their faith or walk someone through the steps of salvation. Personal relationship witnessing needs to be incorporated into the life of a church so that church members are constantly reminded they are called to be involved in sharing their faith. The majority of the unchurched have been and will be reached through personal relationship witnessing.

## Begin Where the Unchurched Are

Churches treat people in one of two ways. They assume that the person is either (1) a knowledgeable, well-informed Christian or (2) a heathen with no religious inclinations whatsoever. Not everyone outside the church, or within the church for that matter, fits into these two categories. Rather, most people fit somewhere in the middle. James Engel[2] has developed the following continuum on which a person's religious development can be assessed. Based on the religiosity of the unchurched, most would fall within the categories of items 3–8.

### Engel's Scale

**Pre-Conversion**

-Has only a superficial awareness of God
-Has faith that there is a supreme being
-Believes he/she is responsible to God
-Realizes he/she is a sinner
-Recognizes that Christ is the bridge to God and his/her salvation
-Realizes sin keeps him/her from salvation
-Is willing to repent and accept Christ

**Conversion**

-Salvation/conversion experience
-Accepts Christ as Savior

**Post-Conversion**

-Publically acknowledges faith/conversion (in church or among friends)
-Faithfully participates in church worship, study groups, or Sunday School
-Participates in discipleship training
-Actively shares his/her faith
-Accepts and is working toward God's design for the family and home
-Personal finances are based on biblical stewardship
-Uses his/her spiritual gifts in local church ministry
-Observes regular personal devotions and prayer
-Becomes Christlike

These levels are where churches need to focus their programming and outreach to the unchurched. Paul reminded some of the Corinthians that they were not ready for the meat of the gospel:

> And so, brothers and sisters, I could not speak to you as spiritual people, but rather as people of the flesh, as infants in Christ. I fed you with milk, not solid food, for you were not ready for solid food. (1 Cor 3:1-2)

A church needs to provide both milk and meat for the people to whom it ministers.

The unchurched want to grow spiritually, but they lack the guidance and means. The following is a list of possible programming and outreach tools churches can employ that focus on the basic religious development of the unchurched. The purposes of these programming and outreach tools are (1) to begin where the unchurched are so that they are not treated as heathens nor mature Christians and (2) to provide the best opportunities in order to assist the unchurched in their religious development.

•Provide a Bible study class that deals with the basics of the Christian faith and biblical knowledge. The teacher of this study should be trained in determining where people are in their religious development. The teacher should be sensitive to presenting the information at the appropriate levels.

•Personal witness training should provide church members with information on determining where the unchurched are in their religious development. As church members begin to practice lifestyle evangelism, they will need to know where the people with whom they are working are on the continuum.

•Provide a prescribed discipleship program for new members, especially new Christians, that will assist them in moving along the religious development continuum.

•An early worship service or a seeker service needs to gear the message and presentation to the childish Christian. Here I am using Paul's idea that we all begin as childish Christians and as we grow spiritually we can put away childish things.

•Offer video and audio tapes that can be viewed by nonchurchgoers at home so they can progress at their own pace.

•Offer seminars on prayer, scripture reading, and personal devotions to instill the importance of religious practices. Many nonchurchgoers do not have a personal devotion/scripture reading time because they have found it unproductive. Seminars can offer tools for developing an effective private devotional time.

## Develop a Market Attitude

If the society outside our walls truly has become unrecognizable by the church, then it is because Christians have been unwilling to take a look at it. A number of reasons exist for why we choose not to notice the change around us: We do not want to become like the world, our worlds outside the church are changing too fast, we want something to stay the same, and the church seems like a safe haven from the world. Whatever the reason is for your church, it is probably very valid. The church does not need to become like the world. The church does need to provide grounding and familiarity for its members whose other worlds are changing drastically. The church can provide a safe haven from the harshness of the world. But the church cannot do only these things. The church must balance its traditions and familiarity with a market attitude.

Churches must develop market attitudes. Please note, I said a market attitude—not a marketing attitude. Marketing is part of the market attitude, but the market attitude is much broader. Businesses live and die on whether or not they develop a market attitude. Many churches have reached the same point. Now I know that most people cringe when they hear the words "market" and "church" in the same sentence, yet Paul had a "market attitude." In 1 Corinthians 9:19-23, he wrote,

> For though I am free with respect to all, I have made myself a slave to all, so that I might win more of them. To the Jews I became as a Jew, in order to win Jews. To those are under the law I became as one under the law (though I myself am not under the law) so that I might win those under the law. To those outside the law I became as one outside the law (though I am not free from God's law but am under Christ's law) so that I might win those outside the law. To the weak I became weak, so that I might win the weak. I have become all things to all people, that I might by all means save some. I do it all for the sake of the gospel, so that I may share in its blessings.

Paul's ultimate goal was to win people to Jesus, and he was prepared to use any means in order that he "might win some." He did not cheapen the gospel by making it and himself appealing to different groups of people. Paul did all that he did for the "sake of the gospel." He had a "market attitude."

Developing a market attitude does not mean that a church must throw out its traditions or traditional style of running the church. It does not mean that the church must forget its past and be something different than what it truly is. The doctrines and beliefs of a church are at no risk whatsoever from developing a market attitude. A local church should never change its doctrine, beliefs, or theology in order to have people join.

Churches, however, must develop a market attitude in order to compete. The vitality of the American Christian scene can directly be attributed to the competitive market of its churches. Churches may see other churches as their only competition. I do not advocate churches competing with each other, but I do advocate churches competing against the world. The world possesses the greatest competition for churches. Unless churches begin to develop market attitudes, then the world will win because it has a great market attitude. This market attitude should include these four components: (1) awareness of reality, (2) flexibility, (3) marketing strategy, and (4) planning.

## Awareness of Reality

A local church must be constantly aware of its surroundings. Many times a local church will practice "blanket ministry." Blanket ministry is where generic programs developed at the denominational level are deposited on a church and its community with no regard for the needs of individuals or groups or agencies within that community. A new program is developed in a urban area by professional people and sent to a rural church whose membership consists mainly of farmers who implement the program for its community of blue collar workers. They might as well write "bust" on the box. Churches require a "needs-based ministry." Needs-based ministry occurs when community analysis informs the church of the needs of individuals, groups, and agencies in the community and from that information ministry is developed. With needs-based ministry, the farmers in the blue-collar town take what is sent from the urban professionals and transform it into a program that will address the needs of their community and church.

Community analysis contains several components: historical knowledge, functions and dysfunctions of the community, knowledge of the economic system (basically where do people work), and community demographics. A church should conduct a community analysis on the average of every four years. Obviously, churches in fast-growing areas should perform an analysis more frequently, and churches in slow-growing areas should perform an analysis less frequently.

### Flexibility

The organizational structure of many churches lacks flexibility. Certain programs or events become icons. Certain committees become entrenched. Normally, this inflexibility is due to the lack of initiative or planning or to stubbornness or ignorance. The members either do not care or do not want to change the program/committee, or they do not realize they should.

A church in this post-modern era must be flexible. It must develop an organizational structure that can change with the shifting realities around it. It must be able to adapt in order to remain proactive and up-to-date in its presentation of the gospel. I offer two suggestions for developing a flexible organizational structure: zero-based budgeting and task forces.

Zero-based budgeting means that at the beginning of the budgeting process for the new year, all line items drop to zero. There is no rolling over of the budget. There is no looking at what you spent the last year and adding 2%. Zero-based budgeting requires the fourth component of a market attitude: planning. Ministry areas, service areas, facilities and maintenance must all submit budgets based on what they plan to do in the coming year. Zero-based budgeting eliminates many of the line-item icons that have become permanent fixtures in many church budgets.

Task forces take the place of many church standing committees. A church will always need standing committees to address permanent needs such as personnel, finance, and ordinances. Many committees, however, should be dissolved every year. Again, planning is the key. The local church must have a clear vision of what it wants to accomplish in the next year. Task forces are then formed around those objectives. Task forces also will eliminate a problem that has plagued churches for years: getting members to serve on committees. Persons are motivated to serve on a task force because (1) it lasts for only one to two years, and (2) the members are given a list of objectives their task force is expected to accomplish.

People hate to waste their time serving on committees that do nothing. They are more likely to say yes when they know that they will be accomplishing something and not just meeting.

## Marketing

A marketing strategy applies to those first impressions a church makes. Here is where the church meets the unchurched, and a well-developed marketing strategy helps make the first impression a good one. In his book, *Marketing the Church: What They Never Taught You about Church Growth*, George Barna lays out an excellent marketing strategy for churches. Barna used a model developed by E. Jerome McCarthy in which he lays out the "Four P's" of marketing: product, place, promotion, and price.

The church delivers many products, both tangible and intangible. The most obvious intangible and most important product is the good news of Jesus Christ. The ministry programs of the church are some of its tangible products. Place "concerns distribution, getting the product to the right place for the right audience."[3] Normally when Christians think of distributing their product, they think of the church. Even though the church is the primary place from which distribution occurs, place must be more than just the church. Promotion is something most churches do not do well. Bringing in someone from a state or national denomination agency to assist with marketing promotion is a great idea.

If promotion is rarely done in churches, price is never thought of. Christians do not associate their product, place, or promotion with price, but the unchurched do. Again the church must realize the reality in which it operates. People are very concerned with investments nowadays. They expect good returns on their money. Businesses give annual reports on production to stockholders. Why shouldn't churches do the same? How effective was that senior adult event? What ever came of the money invested in the youth mission project? Did the Christmas pageant achieve the results we sought? Price and accountability are becoming more important issues for nonprofit organizations—just ask the United Way and higher education.

## Planning

It has always amazed me that church members who run businesses, hold professional positions, or are employed by factories that have quality teams seem to forget all of their business sense when they enter the church. It is as though they have never heard of planning, even though most of them do it in their jobs every day. If a church incorporates none of the other three components of a market attitude, it must plan. Planning is absolutely essential if a church is to be effective. Long-range planning is necessary. Annual planning is essential. A church that does not plan will continue to offer the same mediocre programs, events, and ministry year after year.

Pastors, please listen to this statement by George Barna: "Ultimately, many people judge the pastor not on his ability to preach, teach, or counsel, but on his capacity to make the church run smoothly and efficiently."[4] In 1991, the Southern Baptist Theological Seminary conducted a survey of more than 3,000 Southern Baptist lay leaders to discover qualities necessary for good pastoral leadership. In a segment of the survey, scenarios were to be read that highlighted a particular aspect of pastoral leadership. One scenario pictured the pastor as being a strong evangelist or powerful example of faith and witness.

As the data began to accumulate, a fellow researcher and I guessed the rank of each scenario. At the top we listed the scenarios that highlighted the pastor as having strong relational skills, being a good preacher, and projecting a strong example of faith and witness. At the bottom of the list we noted the administrator. Guess which role came out on top? Administrator. We puzzled and puzzled over this. It did not match the rest of our information. Why would a strong administrator be seen as the top leadership quality?

We began to reread the scenarios very closely. What we discovered supports Barna's statement. The scenarios that received the lowest scores emphasized one particular characteristic of pastoral leadership but contained the statement that because the pastor was so involved in the highlighted characteristic, some things in the church "did not get done." The administrator scenario stated that the pastor was average at all those other leadership qualities, but "things around the church get done." That is what the lay leadership wanted to hear. Planning is essential if a pastor and a church hope to "get things done."

## Balance Ministerial Servanthood and Authority

In his book, *Becoming a Christian Leader,* Ernie White discusses two dimensions of Christian leadership: servanthood and authority. These two dimensions are evident in the life of Jesus. Jesus expressed his concept of servanthood by using the example of the shepherd. The servant leader is one "whose whole life is committed to the well-being of the followers."[5] No matter how the world may change around us, ministers must be foremost servants of God. Pastors may choose to run the church as a CEO, but unless they first exemplify the attitude of a servant, then they have failed in their ministry. Having the attitude of a servant is the foundation on which the rest of a minister's leadership is built. The number-one quality people expect in their pastors is that the pastor be an example of faith and witness. Part of being such an example is being an identified servant of God.

Jesus also demonstrated authority in his ministry. It was plainly evident in his life, his teachings, and his ministry. Authority is the right to do something. It differs from power, which is the ability to do something. Jesus as the Son of God had the right to teach and heal in the name of God. According to White, authority "comes from a clear sense of responsibility." The pastoral leadership should have a clear sense of their responsibilities to the church, its members, and God. Pastors also should exercise the right to use that authority in order to carry out their responsibilities.

A minister's leadership needs to express an appropriate balance of servanthood and authority. According to White,

> To be a guide (and not advisor or dictator), a leader must be ready to serve those guided. Likewise, a guide must be capable (*and willing*) of using appropriate authority to provide direction.[6]

Upon this foundation a minister must build a style of leadership. The linchpins of leadership for Christian ministers are flexibility, consistency, balance, and discernment. Consistency does not mean that ministers should have only one leadership style. Their leadership style should be flexible. It should shift based on the situation and context in which they find themselves. The consistency comes when the situation and context occur again. Ministers are able to maintain this flexible consistency through balance and discernment. Balance allows ministers to be able to effortlessly move between situations and contexts, never leaning toward extremes. Discernment allows ministers to successfully determine which leadership style to use in a given situation or context.

So what is the ministerial leadership model for dealing with the unchurched? The modern world expects professionalism, leadership, and expertise. Howard F., a younger executive type, said,

> *The church is a joke. It is using 1950 methods and procedures in the twenty-first century. Since it is using outdated methods, then it itself*

*must be outdated. Preachers may be good at preaching, but they are*
*lousy at running an organization. If churches were businesses, they*
*would go bankrupt in months.*

Churches are not businesses, but Howard's point does strike near the
heart of the matter. A ministerial staff must be competent in their duties
and able to effectively carry out the role for which they have been hired.
Remember, the key phrase is "gets the job done." Add to this that "the
job" must be high quality work, which requires planning and promotion.
Unless they serve on a large multiple staff, ministers must become gener-
alists and not specialists. Ministers cannot specialize in preaching or
teaching or evangelism. They are expected to do all of those things and
do them well, especially pastors or senior ministers. Being a generalist
does not mean that a minister must have average skills in many areas.
Rather, a generalist must be highly competent in many areas.

Another reality of the unchurched and their reflection of the modern
world is that ministers are seen as experts in their field and are sought
after as experts. Such a reality grates against the theological nerves of ministers. Ministers have perceived their theological calling to be one of
enabling people in their faith journeys—not one of directing, guiding, or
telling. Yet the unchurched view ministers as they view physicians or
lawyers—as people who have knowledge that can help them.

When I go to see my physician, I do not debate with him over a
diagnosis. I do not question the prescription my physician prescribes. I
may seek another opinion, but it is from another physician. Senior pastors, especially, must preach, teach, and lead with authority. The
unchurched have developed an attitude of wanting to be told what to
believe and how to find fulfillment. Whether this attitude is right or
wrong or theologically correct is not the issue. It is the way things are in
our society. The unchurched have attributed to ministers authority in the
area of spiritual and church matters. Ministers must be willing to use that
authority.

Listen to the words of John K., a foreman at a large factory.

*I make decisions every minute of the day while I am at work. I come*
*home, and there are more decisions about money and chores and*
*family to be made. When I go to church, I do not want to have to*
*make a another decision about some theological question. I want the*
*preacher to tell me the way it is. I mean, that's his job. That's what*
*he is trained to do.*

The unchurched want ministers to show them the way to abundant life and give them directions on how to get there. Remember, the picture of balanced leadership is the guide. One reason conservative and fundamentalist churches are growing—especially among young, educated, business-type people—is because they are fulfilling this need. Preaching, teaching, and leading with authority do not signal that a pastor becomes dictatorial or even an authoritarian. Jesus balanced authority with servanthood. The unchurched are looking for what they saw in Jesus: a servant who spoke "with authority." The modern world expects ministers to be experts and to share their expertise.

## Care for Children

The majority of nonchurchgoers will try to reconnect to the church during critical maturing events in their lives. The most common reconnection time is when they have young children. They are looking for help in trying to establish in their children a set of values and morals; therefore, they look to the church. The church must be ready to assist these parents in the task or miss a great opportunity to affect the lives of both their children and themselves.

Churches must make taking care of the children a priority, but for some reason we do not. In fact, it is almost an afterthought for most churches. Children's ministry is something we just normally "do" without much focused thought. In all fairness, churches "do" an adequate job of it through Sunday School, Vacation Bible School, and other children's activities. Yet here we have the opportunity to influence the return of many nonchurchgoers, and we continue to "do" it as an afterthought. When a church is able to hire multiple staff, when do the children get consideration? Normally after the hiring of the minister of music, the minister of education, and the minister to youth. How many churches can afford a staff like that?

Yet no matter how many staff members a church has or does not have, it must begin making ministry to children and their families a priority. Parents are concerned in today's world about the security of their children. Ministry events must be conducted in a safe environment and manner. The ministry events must be of high quality as well, because both parents and children can spot a shoddy program. The program must be lively and entertaining—we are up against Barney, the Power Rangers, Street Fighter, and MTV. All in all, it comes down to the simple rule: "Parents will go where the children want to go."

Taking care of the children may mean some upscale entertaining, but it can also be a time when a church shapes the values, morals, and attitudes of the next generation. Nonchurchgoing parents are searching for value training and moral education for their children. Studies show that the large majority of parents outside the church who are now wanting their children to have religious training also had it when they were children. Taking care of the children must cease being an afterthought and become a priority if we are going to reach this generation of unchurched . . . and the next.

## Strive for Quality

One of the major hindrances to most churches today is the maintenance of mediocrity. Our churches have become places where one can find mediocre promotion of mediocre programs conducted with mediocre effort. Why is this the case? Why hasn't there been an outcry to improve the quality of our church worship, programming, and ministry?

I refer to the illustration popularized by George Barna in his book, *The Frog and the Kettle.* For many decades, the church was the only game in town. It was the center of the community, the social outlet for the people. If something was happening in town, it was happening at the church. Add to this the self-denial ethic during the period that imprinted on the minds and hearts of the people that when the church doors were open, you had better be there. The local church held a monopoly on the social, educational, and wellness domain of people's lives. Under such circumstances the local church did not have to produce what today we would consider high quality events. The people had no other choice, nor did the people expect as much. Therefore the church did its thing, and the people came.

As the decades passed, the expectations of the people began to rise. The institutions and domains around the people began not only to remove some of the church's previous responsibilities, but raise them to a higher level of quality. People began to expect higher and higher quality. Therefore politics, business, education, health care, and recreation began to deliver higher levels of quality out of the necessity to compete. But like the frog in the kettle who will comfortably cook himself to death if the water is heated gradually, churches have failed to take heed of this rising expectation. Again, I am amazed that churchgoers who expect high quality in every other area of their lives allow the church to operate at a mediocre level. I do know some churchgoers who have not allowed this and have sought out those churches that are not cooking to death in the oil of mediocrity.

Churches must begin quality improvement strategies at once. We have already discussed the need for a market attitude. Churches must be aware of their realities, be flexible, and plan and promote. In turn, the programs, events, promotion, and leadership must be of high quality, or the market attitude is worthless. The market attitude may get the people to your church once, but quality will keep them. Consider the following suggestions for quality improvement.

## Promotion

Any promotional material that leaves your church—be it a newsletter, an article for the newspaper, or a promotional poster—should be printed and of professional design. You do not have to pay someone to professionally design your promotional materials. Find the creative people in your church. Use computer desktop publishing software.

The days of the last minute, handwritten poster are over. A business friend of mine in Kentucky was complaining about our church's use of handwritten posters to advertise events. "Ron, you know what that says to me?" referring to the poster on the wall. "It says first that this event is going to be on the same caliber quality-wise as that poster and second that whoever is in charge of this event has not planned well enough, so at the last minute, handwritten posters was the quickest thing to do."

Printing is expensive indeed. Last year the business world spent billions of dollars in printed advertisements. But a printed poster or brochure speaks volumes about the quality of the event and the effort put into it. If you cannot promote every event this way, you should consider (1) reducing the number of events you sponsor, (2) spending more money on printing, or (3) at least selecting several key events to promote in a professional way.

## Programming

Churchgoers and nonchurchgoers will attend events at church that they believe will be worthwhile. Concerts, seminars, churchwide gatherings, and musical performances should be of high quality. Once a church offers substandard events, it is hard for that church to continue to attract people to its programs. On the other hand, when a church offers high quality programming, the church will attract not only its own members but the unchurched as well.

Church members and the community need to be informed in advance about regular programming events such as Bible study, discipleship development, and worship. What are the upcoming topics? What issues will the worship service address? Churches have never had to promote their programming in such a way, but in today's society where time is precious, such promotion is imperative.

"Worthwhileness" is determined not only by the content of an event, but by the way the event is delivered. Consider these guidelines:

•Do not throw together an event at the last minute; people can tell.

•Do not try to fill every position with a warm body. Use only qualified persons to teach, lead, direct, or serve. Limit your programming to the number of qualified individuals you have. If you need qualified individuals, then develop a leadership training program.

•Be more intentional about linking leaders up with their strengths. I have heard it said too often, "Well, she is a good teacher. I'm sure she would be a good administrator." People possess different gifts; discover those gifts

•When enlisting teachers or program leaders, lay down expectations of quality. What level of quality does the church expect of this program? Can the person provide that level of quality given his or her present time constraints and abilities?

•Provide the programming leaders with the best structural support possible. Structural support refers to room setting, room decor, visual and audio equipment, teaching aids, and so on.

## Leadership

We have already discussed how the ministerial staff of a church must be seen as experts in their fields. They can no longer merely possess the credentials of ministers; they must possess the qualities of pastoral leaders. A church can no longer depend on a popularity vote or the church's power structure to select leaders. Lay leadership must be developed and then chosen and placed according to the leadership abilities they possess. Such a system does not mean that the pastor can fill the leadership positions of the church with only supporters or that church members cannot select their leaders. It means that church members need to be better informed of leadership needs and expectations so they can make informed decisions. Lay leadership training and development is essential for any church. Leaders may be born, but they can also be made.

## Adjust Scheduling

All institutions are greedy. They want to possess individuals—their time, their talents, and their resources. Most institutions will operate under an assumption that those within the institution have no other commitments. Churches are no different. Churches ask for all of the above. Yet time (or the lack of it) is the major reason many persons do not attend church. Since this is the case, churches must seriously address the issue of scheduling and discover better ways to make "church" fit into the schedules of the unchurched.

I hear a voice from the back of the crowd scream, "If they were committed, then they would make time for the church." That's right, and if churchgoers were committed, then 80% of the church's work would be done by 80% of the members and not the actual 20% of members. Most of the "committed" churchgoers give one hour a week to church. How can the local church increase not only the participation and involvement of nonchurchgoers, but also that of the vast majority of churchgoers who attend only the Sunday morning worship hour? Are we seeking to make mere attenders out of the nonchurchgoers, or are we wanting them to be faithful members?

The issue of scheduling should address three areas: (1) getting them in; (2) keeping them involved; and (3) more impact, less time. Getting them in involves planning events that fit the schedules of the unchurched. Each church must analyze its own community context to determine such times. Does your community have a large number of shift workers? Do many people commute to work and therefore arrive home late in the evening? Do you have a large number of young families with children?

I once consulted with a pastor who was bemoaning a recent event at his church that had fallen flat. He talked about how the staff had promoted the event well in advance. They had publicized it in a very professional way. They had secured good entertainment and a well-known speaker. It was addressing an expressed desire of the church. But when the event came, the turnout was miserable. I asked a series of questions and got nowhere. Then I remembered seeing a large automobile plant on my way into town. I asked if the pastor had checked the plant's calendar. He said "no" as a wave of enlightenment crossed his face.

Slowly, he picked up the phone and called the plant. I heard him ask if they had something scheduled the night of the event. A brief pause and then a few pleasantries were exchanged. As the receiver was placed back in its resting place, he looked at me with a dejected look and said, "The plant had a family picnic that day. It didn't conflict with our event, but I guess the people were too tired to go back out that evening."

In a busy world, churches must be concerned about the other lives of the unchurched and of their own church members. Scheduling of church events must fit into their lives.

Keeping people involved in the church means avoiding the monopolization of their time. The church is one of the greediest institutions. "My family was in church every time the doors were open" is still an expectation of the church. When that saying originated, the church was all the people had to do outside of work. That is no longer the case, and yet churches have maintained that expectation. Many persons do not attend church because they were unwilling to give the time expected by the church. The church does have a right to expect its members to be committed and to participate in church events (so long as the church is committed to offering quality events), but the church also must schedule events in a more economical manner.

I looked back at this past year and what I did at church as a layperson. There were literally weeks and weeks that I could have attended something at church every day or night. Why? Because churches appear to be oblivious to the other commitments of people. When I schedule events as a minister for my church, I try to schedule them on three nights: Sunday, Wednesday, and one other night of the week. Normally at my church people are there on Sunday and Wednesday, so most training sessions, committee meetings, and other "maintenance" activities occur on those nights. Special events that occur sporadically are scheduled on the other night of the week. I am still concerned that even this is too much. Churches must be more economical about their scheduling in order to keep people involved.

More impact, less time means becoming more economical *about* time and more effective *with* time. We not only need to be more economical about scheduling, but we also need to be more economical about the amount of time we schedule. If an event can take thirty minutes, why make it an hour? If the purposes of a program can be accomplished in two hours, why schedule half a day? By making the amount of time more economical, we should increase the effectiveness of using that time. It makes the leader of an event more responsible for effectively and efficiently managing the allotted time.

Please pardon a brief excursion. Meetings are the bane of the modern world. I do not dislike meetings, but I despise a poorly-run meeting. You know—the kind in which you sit for an hour or more and walk away wondering what was accomplished and what else you could have been doing with your time. Church committee meetings are the worst. First, church committee chairs should be trained in scheduling and conducting effective and efficient meetings. There must be a reason for meeting and a stated purpose to accomplish. There needs to be a time-tied agenda—so many minutes for each topic, with the leader facilitating a balance between input and time. Whatever we do as churches, we must develop an attitude of creating more impact in less time.

## A Final Challenge

The unchurched are becoming the common religious component of American society. Their spiritual lives represent the spiritual attitude of society. Religious faith is a private matter, decided on between the individual and God. The unchurched also represent the common feeling of American society toward the church in general. They do not rave against Christianity but against the mockery made of Christianity by visible church leaders and the apparent lack of spirituality within churches. The unchurched have not abandoned Christianity, but they no longer connect with the religious symbolism used by most churches.

Churches must begin to transform themselves so that they may present the powerful and timely message of Jesus Christ in a modern, up-to-date method. The New Testament clearly demonstrates that Jesus wrapped the gospel in everyday, human ingredients: objects, symbols, and words that were familiar to the people around him. Churches must not only transform themselves in reaction to the changing realities of our society; they must also recapture their role as shapers of our society.

We Christians no longer can allow the forces of the world to dictate our destiny. We possess the most powerful shaper of culture and history the world has ever known in the message of Jesus Christ. We must become proactive in shaping the growing spirituality in our nation. The unchurched are searching for religious and spiritual answers. They are searching for a place on which to ground and grow their faith. Many are willing and wanting to return to such a place. The harvest is ripe, but the harvest will come only if churches can adapt to the challenge.

## Notes

[1]Byang H. Kato, "The Gospel, Cultural Context, and Religious Syncretism," in *Let the Earth Hear His Voice*, ed. J. D. Douglas (Minneapolis MN: World Wide, 1975) 1217. For a full discussion on the topic of contextualization, see David J. Hesselgrave and Edward Rommen, *Contextualization: Meanings, Methods, and Models* (Grand Rapids MI: Baker Book House, 1989).

[2]James E. Engel, *What's Gone Wrong with the Harvest?* as quoted in Larry Gilbert, *Team Evangelism* (Lynchburg VA: Church Growth Institute, 1991) 95.

[3]George Barna, *Marketing the Church: What They Never Taught You about Church* Growth (Colorado Springs CO: NavPress, 1990) 43.

[4]Ibid., 14.

[5]Ernest White, *Becoming a Servant Leader* (Nashville TN: Convention Press, 1985) 24.

[6]Ibid., 33.

# BIBLIOGRAPHY

**Books**

Anderson, James D. *To Come Alive! A New Proposal for Revitalizing the Local Church*. New York: Harper & Row, 1973.

Antonio, Robert J., and Ronald M. Glassman, eds. *A Weber-Marx Dialogue*. Lawrence KA: University Press of Kansas, 1985.

Arieli, Yehoshua. *Individualism and Nationalism in American Ideology*. Cambridge MA: Harvard University Press, 1964.

Ashley, David, and David M. Orenstein. *Sociological Theory: Classical Statements*. Boston: Allyn and Bacon, 1990.

Aulect, Roger, ed. *Sacralization and Secularization*. New York: Paulist Press, 1969.

Ausmus, Harry J. *The Polite Escape: On the Myth of Secularization*. Athens OH: Ohio University Press, 1982.

Bakke, Ray. *The Urban Christian*. Downers Grove IL: Intervarsity Press, 1987.

Barna, George. *The Frog in the Kettle*. Ventura CA: Regal Books, 1990.

_____. *Marketing the Church: What They Never Taught You about Church Growth*. Colorado Springs CO: Navpress, 1990.

Bellah, Robert. *Beyond Belief*. New York: Harper & Row, 1970.

_____. *The Broken Covenant*. New York: Seabury Press, 1975.

_____. "Christian Faithfulness in a Pluralistic World." In *Postmodern Theology: The Church in a Pluralistic World*. Ed. Frederick B. Burnham. New York: Harper & Row, 1989.

_____ et al. *Habits of the Heart: Individualism and Commitment in American Life*. New York: Harper & Row, 1985.

_____ and Phillip Hammond. *Varieties of Civil Religion*. San Francisco: Harper & Row, 1980.

Bender, Thomas. *Community and Social Change in America*. Baltimore MD: John Hopkins University Press, 1978.

Berger, J., M. Zelditch, and B. Anderson. *Sociological Theory in Progress*, vol. 2. Boston: Houghton-Mifflin, 1972.

Berger, Peter. *Facing Up to Modernity: Excursions in Society, Politics, and Religion*. New York: Basic Books Inc., 1977.

_____. *The Rumor of Angels*. Garden City NY: Doubleday, 1969.

_____. *The Sacred Canopy: Elements of a Sociological Theory of Religion*. New York: Anchor Books, 1969.

_____ and Thomas Luckmann. *The Social Construction of Reality: A Treatise in the Sociology of Knowledge*. New York: Anchor Press, 1967.

Bruce, Steve. *A House Divided: Protestantism, Schism, and Secularization*. London: Routledge, 1990.

Campbell, Colin. *Toward a Sociology of Irreligion*. London: Macmillan, 1971.

Caplovitz, David, and Fred Sherrow. *The Religious Dropouts: Apostasy among College Graduates*. Beverly Hills CA: Sage Publications, 1977.

Caplow, Theodore, Howard M. Bahr, and Bruce A. Chadwick. *All Faithful People*. Minneapolis MN: University of Minnesota Press, 1983.

Carroll, Jackson W., Douglas W. Johnson, and Martin E. Marty. *Religion in America: 1950 to Present*. New York: Harper & Row, 1979.

Childress, James F., and David B. Harned, eds. *Secularization and the Protestant Prospect*. Philadelphia: Westminster Press, 1970.

Clanton, Gordon. *Peter L. Berger and the Reconstruction of the Sociology of Religion*. Ann Arbor MI: University Microfilms, 1973.

Cox, Harvey. *The Secular City*. New York: MacMillan, 1965.

de Tocqueville, Alexis. *Democracy in America*. Trans. G. Lawrence. New York: Doubleday, Anchor Books, 1969.

Dobbelaere, Karel. *Secularization*. London: Sage Publications, 1981.

Douglass, H. Paul, and Edmund de S. Brunner. *The Church as a Social Institution*. New York: Harper, 1935.

DuBose, Francis. *How Churches Grow in an Urban World*. Nashville: Broadman Press, 1978.

Dudley, Carl S., ed. *Building Effective Ministry: Theory and Practice in the Local Church*. San Francisco: Harper & Row, 1983.

Durkheim, Emile. *Division of Labor in Society*. Trans. George Simpson. Glencoe IL: The Free Press, 1949.

_____. *The Elementary Forms of Religious Life*. Trans. Joseph Ward Swain. New York: The Free Press, 1949.

_____. "Individualism and the Intellectuals." In *Emile Durkheim: On Morality and Society*. Ed. R. Bellah. Chicago: University of Chicago Press, 1973.

_____. *The Rules of Sociological Method and Selected Texts on Sociology and Its Method*. Trans. W. D. Halls. New York: The Free Press, 1982.

Earle, John R., Dean D. Knudsen, and Donald A. Shiver, Jr. *Spindles and Spires*. Atlanta: John Knox Press, 1976.

Edwards, David L. *Religion and Change*. New York: Harper & Row, 1969.

Faulding, Harold. *The Sociology of Religion*. Toronto: McGraw-Hill Ryeison Limited, 1974.

Fenn, Richard K. *Toward a Theory of Secularization*. Ellington CT: K & R Printer, Inc., 1978.

Finney, Charles. *Sermons on Important Subjects*. New York: John S. Taylor, 1836.

Fischer, Claude. *The Urban Experience*. San Diego: Harcourt Brace Jovanovich, 1984.

_____. *To Dwell among Friends: Personal Network in Town and City*. Chicago: University of Chicago Press, 1982.

Fleming, Bruce C. E. *Contextualization of Theology: An Evangelical Assessment*. Pasadena CA: William Carey Library, 1980.

Frank, Douglas. *Less Than Conquers: How Evangelicals Entered the Twentieth Century*. Grand Rapids MI: Eerdmans, 1986.

Gallup, George. *The Unchurched American*. Princeton NJ: Princeton Religion Research Center, 1978.

_____. *The Unchurched American . . . 10 Years Later*. Princeton NJ: Princeton Religion Research Center, 1988.

Garrearu, Joel. *The Nine Nations of North America*. Boston: Houghton Mifflin, 1981.

Glasner, Peter. *The Sociology of Secularization: A Critique of a Concept*. London: Routledge & Kegan Paul, 1977.

Glock, Charles, and Rodney Stark. *American Piety*. Berkeley CA: University of California Press, 1968.

_____, and Robert Bellah. *The New Religious Consciousness*. Berkeley CA: University of California Press, 1976.

_____, ed. *Religion in Sociological Perspective: Essays in the Empirical Study of Religion*. Belmont CA: Wadsworth, 1973.

Greeley, Andrew. *Catholic Schools in a Declining Church*. Kansas City MO: Sheed & Ward, 1976.

Hadaway, C. Kirk, and Wade Clark Roof. "Apostasy in American Churches: Evidence from National Survey Data." In *Falling from the Faith: Causes and Consequences of Religious Apostasy*. Ed. David G. Bromley. London: Sage Publications, 1988.

Hale, J. Russell. *The Unchurched: Who They Are and Why They Stay Away*. San Francisco: Harper & Row, 1977.

Hargrove, Barbara. *The Sociology of Religion: Classical and Contemporary Approaches*. Arlington Heights IL: AHM, 1979.

Herberg, Will. *Protestant, Catholic, Jew: An Essay in American Sociology.* Garden City NY: Doubleday, 1955.

Hesselgrave, David J., and Edward Rommen. *Contextualization: Meanings, Methods, and Models.* Grand Rapids MI: Baker Book House, 1989.

Hill, Michael. *The Sociology of Religion.* London: Heineann Educational Books, 1973.

Hoge, Dean R. *Commitment on Campus: Changes in Religion and Values over Five Decades.* Philadelphia: Westminster Press, 1974.

_____. *Converts, Dropouts, and Returnees: A Study of Religious Change among Catholics.* New York: Pilgrim Press, 1981.

_____. *Division in the Protestant House: The Basic Reasons behind Intra-Church Conflicts.* Philadelphia: Westminster Press, 1976.

_____, and David A. Roozen, eds. *Understanding Church Growth and Decline: 1950–1978.* New York: Pilgrim Press, 1981.

Hopewell, James F. *Congregations: Stories and Structures.* Philadelphia: Fortress Press, 1987.

Johnson, James E. *The Life of Charles Grandison Finney.* Ann Arbor MI: University Microfilms International, 1980.

Johnstone, Ronald L. *Religion and Society in Interaction: The Sociology of Religion.* Englewood Cliffs NJ: Pentice-Hill, 1980.

Kato, Byang H. "The Gospel, Cultural Context, and Religious Syncretism." In *Let the Earth Hear His Voice.* Ed. J. D. Douglas. Minneapolis MN: World Wide Publishers, 1975.

Keefe, Donald J. *Thomism and the Ontological Theology of Paul Tillich: A Comparison of Systems.* Leiden: F. J. Brill, 1971.

Lauer, Robert H. *Perspectives on Social Change.* 3rd ed. Boston: Allyn & Bacon, 1982.

Leon, Arnold E. *Secularization: Science Without God?* London: SCM, 1965.

Lifton, Robert Jay. *Boundaries: Psychological Man in Revolution.* New York: Random House, 1970.

Luckmann, Thomas. *The Invisible Religion.* New York: MacMillan, 1967.

Lyons, David. *The Steeple's Shadow: On the Myths and Realities of Secularization.* Grand Rapids MI: Eerdmanns, 1987.

Macquarrie, John. *In Search of Deity: An Essay in Dialectical Theism.* New York: Crossroads, 1985.

_____. *Principles of Christian Theology.* New York: Charles Scribner's Sons, 1977.

Marsden, George. *Fundamentalism and American Culture.* Oxford: Oxford University Press, 1980.

Martin, David. *A General Theory of Secularization.* New York: Harper & Row, 1978.

Marty, Martin. *A Nation of Behavers*. Chicago: University of Chicago Press, 1976.

Mason, Michael. *The Privatization of the Sacred Sphere*. Ann Arbor MI: University Microfilms International, 1984.

Meland, Benard E. *The Secularization of Modern Cultures*. New York: Oxford University Press, 1966.

Merton, Robert K. *Social Theory and Social Structure*. New York: Harper & Row, 1974.

Miller, James B. "The Emerging Postmodern World." In *Postmodern Theology: Christian Faith in a Pluralistic World*. Ed. Frederick B. Burnham. New York: Harper & Row, 1989.

Mills, C. Wright. *The Sociological Imagination*. London: Oxford Univrsity Press, 1959.

Moberg, David O. *The Church as a Social Institution: The Sociology of American Religion*. Grand Rapids MI: Baker Book House, 1962.

Needleman. J., and G. Baker, eds. *Understanding New Religious Movements*. New York: Seabury, 1978.

Neuhaus, Robert John. *The Naked Public Square: Religion and Democracy in America*. Grand Rapids MI: Eerdmans, 1984.

Nicholls, Bruce. *Contextualization: A Theology of Gospel and Culture*. Downers Grove IL: InterVarsity, 1979.

Parsons, Talcott. *The Social System*. Glencoe IL: The Free Press, 1951.

_____. *Theory of Society: Foundations of Modern Sociological Theory*. New York: The Free Press, 1961.

_____. *Social Structure and Personality*. London: Collier-Macmillan, 1970.

_____. *The Systems of Modern Societies*. Englewood Cliffs NJ: Prentice-Hall, 1975.

Pfeffer, Leo. *Creeds in Competition*. New York: Harper, 1958.

Pickering, W. S. F. *Durkheim's Sociology of Religion*. London: Routledge and Kegan Paul, 1984.

Poggi, Gianfranco. *Calvinism and the Capitalist Spirit*. Amherst MA: University of Massachusetts Press, 1983.

Poloma, Margaret. *Contemporary Sociological Theory*. New York: MacMillan, 1979.

Roberts, Keith. *Religion in Sociological Perspective*. 2nd ed. Belmont CA: Wadsworth, 1990.

Roof, Wade Clark, and William McKinney. *American Mainline Religion: Its Changing Shape and Future*. London: Rutgers University Press, 1987.

_____. *Community and Commitment: Religious Plausibility in a Liberal Protestant Church*. New York: Elsevier, 1978.

_____. "Concepts and Indicators of Religious Commitment: A Critical Review." In *The Religious Dimension: New Directions in Quantitative Research*. Ed. Robert Wuthnow. New York: Academe Press, 1979.

Roozen, David A. *The Churched and Unchurched in America*. Washington DC: Glenmary Research Center, 1978.

_____, William McKinney, and Jackson W. Carroll. *Varieties of Religious Presence*. New York: Pilgrim Press, 1984.

Sample, Tex. *U. S. Lifestyles and Mainline Churches: A Key to Reaching People in the 90s*. Louisville KY: Westminster/John Knox Press, 1990.

Schultze, Quentin J., ed. *American Evangelicals and the Mass Media*. Grand Rapids MI: Academie Books, 1990.

_____. *Televangelism and American Culture: The Business of Popular Religion*. Grand Rapids MI: Baker Book House, 1991.

Smith, Harry E. *Secularization and the University*. Richmond VA: John Knox Press, 1968.

Spence, Janet T., et al. *Elementary Statistics*. Englewood Cliffs NJ: Prentice-Hall, 1983.

Stark, Rodney, and William Sims Bainbridge. *The Future of Religion: Secularization, Revival, and Cult Formation*. Berkeley CA: University of California Press, 1985.

Strommen, Merton P., et al. *The Study of Generations*. Minneapolis MN: Augsburg, 1972.

Taber, Charles R. "Hermeneutics and Culture: An Anthropological Perspective." In *Gospel and Culture*. Ed. John R. W. Stott and Robert T. Coote. Pasadena CA: William Carey Library, 1979.

Tillich, Paul. *Dynamics of Faith*. New York: Harper & Row, 1957.

_____. *Systematic Theology*, vol. 1. Chicago: University of Chicago Press, 1951.

Toennes, Ferdinand. *Community and Society*. Trans. C. P. Loomis. New York: Harper, 1963.

Wagner, Helmut R. *Alfred Schultz: An Intellectual Biography*. Chicago: University of Chicago Press, 1983.

Weber, Max. *Economy and Society: An Outline of Interpretive Sociology*. Eds. G. Roth and C. Wittich. New York: Bedminster Press, 1964.

_____. *The Protestant Ethic and the Spirit of Capitalism*. Trans. T. Parsons. New York: Charles Scribner's Sons, 1958.

_____. "Science as Vocation." In *From Max Weber: Essays in Sociology*. Eds. H. H. Gerth and C. W. Mills. New York: Oxford University Press, 1946.

_____. *The Sociology of Religion*. Trans. E. Fischoff. Boston: Beacon Press, 1964.

Wilson, Bryan. *Religion in Secular Society*. Harmondsworth: Penguin Books, 1969.

_____. *Religion in Sociological Perspective*. Oxford: Oxford University Press, 1982.

Winter, Gibson. *The Suburban Captivity of the Churches*. Garden City NY: Doubleday & Co., 1961.

Winter, Jerry Alan. *Continuities in the Sociology of Religion*. New York: Harper & Row, 1977.

Wuthnow, Robert, ed. *The Religious Dimension: New Directions in Quantitative Research*. New York: Academic Press, 1979.

_____. *The Restructuring of American Religion: Society and Faith Since World War II*. Princeton NJ: Princeton University Press, 1987.

_____. *The Struggle for the American Soul: Evangelicals, Liberals, and Secularism*. Grand Rapids MI: Eerdmanns, 1989.

_____., and Robert C. Liebman, eds. *The New Christian Right*. New York: Aldine, 1983.

Yankelovich, Daniel. *New Rules: Searching for Self-Fulfillment in a World Turned Upside Down*. New York: Random House, 1981.

Yinger, Milton. *Religion, Society, and the Individual*. New York: Macmillan, 1957.

_____. *The Scientific Study of Religion*. New York: Macmillan, 1970.

## Periodicals

Albrecht, Stan L., and Howard M. Bahr. "Strangers Once More: Patterns of Disaffiliation from Mormonism." *Journal for the Scientific Study of Religion* 28 (1989): 187.

Beardslee, John W., III. "Secularization." *Reformed Review* 22 (1969): 51.

Bellah, Robert. "Christianity and Symbolic Realism." *Journal for the Scientific Study of Religion* 9 (1970): 93.

_____. "Discerning Old and New Imperatives in Theological Education." *Theological Education* 19 (1982): 12.

_____. "Religious Evolution." *American Sociological Review* 29 (1964): 371.

Brinkerhoff, Merlin B., and Kathryn L. Burke. "Disaffiliation: Some Notes on 'Falling from the Faith.' " *Sociological Analysis* 41 (1980): 43.

Clayton, Richard R., and James W. Gladden. "The 5 Dimensions of Religiosity: Toward a Demythologizing of a Sacred Artifact." *Journal for the Scientific Study of Religion* 13 (1974): 142.

Cornwall, Marie, Stan L. Albrecht, Perry H. Cunningham, and Brian L. Pitcher. "The Dimensions of Religiosity: A Conceptual Model with an Empirical Test." *Review of Religious Research* 27 (1986): 226.

Cox, Jeffery. "Secularization and Social History." *Theology* 78 (1975): 91.

Crippen, Timothy. "Old and New Gods in the Modern World: Toward a Theory of Religious Transformation." *Social Forces* 67 (1989): 332.

DeJong, Gordon D., Joseph Faulkner, and R. Warland. "Dimensions of Religiosity Reconsidered: Evidence from a Cross-Cultural Study." *Social Forces* 54 (1976): 866-89.

Dobbelaere, Karel. "Secularization Theories and Sociological Paradigms: Convergence and Divergences." *Social Compass* 31 (1984): 203.

_____. "Secularization Theories and Sociological Paradigms: A Reformulation of the Private-Public Dichotomy and the Problem of Societal Integration." *Sociological Analysis* 46 (1985): 378-81.

_____. "Some Trends in European Sociology of Religion." *Sociological Analysis* 48 (1987): 107-37.

Faulkner, Jospeh E., and Gordon F. DeJong. "Religiosity in 5-D: An Empirical Analysis." *Social Forces* 45 (1966): 246-54.

Feagin, Joe R. "Prejudice and Religious Types: A Focused Study of Southern Fundamentalists." *Journal for the Scientific Study of Religion* 4 (1969): 3-13.

Fenn, Richard K. "The Process of Secularization: A Post-Parsonian View." *Journal for the Scientific Study of Religion* 9 (1970): 135.

Fichter, Joseph H. "Sociological Measures of Religiosity." *Review of Religious Research* 10 (1969): 170.

Firebaugh, Glenn, and Brian Harley. "Trends in U.S. Church Attendance: Secularization and Revival, or Merely Lifecycle Effects?" *Journal for the Scientific Study of Religion* 30 (1991): 487.

Glock, Charles Y. "On the Study of Religious Commitment." *Religious Education: Research Supplement* 57 (1962): 98.

Gorsuch, Richard, and Susan E. McPherson. "Intrinsic/Extrinsic Measurement: I/E Revised." *Journal for the Scientific Study of Religion* 28 (1989): 348-54.

Hadaway, C. Kirk. "Identifying American Apostasy: A Cluster Analysis." *Journal for the Scientific Study of Religion* 28 (1989): 200-231.

Hadden, Jeffery K. "Toward Desacralizing Secularization Theory." *Social Forces* 65 (1987): 590-602.

Harrison, Simon. "Ritual Hierarchy and Secular Equality in a Sepek River Village." *American Ethnologist* 12 (1985): 420.

Hart, Stephen. "Privatization in American Religion and Society." *Sociological Analysis* 47 (1987): 321.

Hoge, Dean R. "A Validated Intrinsic Religious Motivation Scale." *Journal for the Scientific Study of Religion* 11 (1972): 369-76.

Hunsberger, Bruce E. "Apostasy: A Social Learning Perspective." *Review of Religious Research* 25 (1983): 21.

_____. "A Reexamination of the Antecedents of Apostasy." *Review of Religious Research* 21 (1980): 160.

_____. "The Religiosity of College Students: Stability and Change over Years in the University." *Journal for the Scientific Study of Religion* 17 (1978): 159-64.

_____, and L. B. Brown. "Religious Socialization, Apostasy, and the Impact of Family Background." *Journal for the Scientific Study of Religion* 23 (1984): 40-53.

Jacobson, Cardell K., Tim B. Heaton, and Rutledge M. Dennis. "Black-White Differences in Religiosity: Item Analysis and a Formal Structural Test." *Sociological Analysis* 51 (1990): 261.

King, Morton B., and Richard A. Hunt. "Measuring the Religious Variable: Amended Findings." *Journal for the Scientific Study of Religion* 8 (1969) 318-26.

_____. "Measuring the Religious Variable: A National Replication." *Journal for the Scientific Study of Religion* 14 (1975): 13-22.

_____. "Measuring the Religious Variable: Nine Proposed Dimensions." *Journal for the Scientific Study of Religion* 6 (1967): 176.

_____. "Measuring the Religious Variable: Replication." *Journal for the Scientific Study of Religion* 11 (1972): 240-51.

Luckmann, Thomas. "Religion in Modern Society: Individual Consciousness, World View, and Institutions." *Journal for the Scientific Study of Religion* 2 (1963): 153.

_____. "Shrinking Transcendence, Expanding Religion?" *Sociological Analysis* 50 (1990): 134.

Lyons, David. "Rethinking Secularization: Retrospect and Prospect." *Review of Religious Research* 26 (1985): 56.

_____. "Secularization: The Fate of Faith in Modern Society." *Themelios* 10 (1984): 17.

Meuller, G. H. "The Dimensions of Religiosity." *Sociological Analysis* 41 (1980): 1-24.

Mol, J. J. "Secularization and Cohesion." *Review of Religious Research* 11 (1970): 183-91.

Morris, Ronald, and Ralph W. Hood, Jr. "The Generalizability and Specificy of Intrinsic/ Extrinsic Orientations." *Review of Religious Research* 22 (1981) 245-54.

Mount, C. Eric. "American Individualism Reconsidered." *Review of Religious Research* 22 (1981): 364.

Seidman, Steven. "Modernity and the Problem of Meaning: The Durkheimian Tradition." *Sociological Analysis* 46 (1985): 125.

Shiner, Larry L. "The Concept of Secularization in Empirical Research." *Journal for the Scientific Study of Religion* 6 (1967): 207-220.

Smith, Gary Scott. "The Great Secularization Debate in America." *Reformed Journal* 35 (1985): 15-19.

Tamney, Joseph B., and Stephen D. Johnson. "Consequential Religiosity in Modern Society." *Review of Religious Research* 26 (1985): 360-78.

Thomson, Irene Taviss. "The Transformation of the Social Bond: Images of Individualism in the 1920s versus the 1970s." *Social Forces* 67 (1989): 853.

Tschannen, Olivier. "The Secularization Paradigm: A Systematization." *Journal for the Scientific Study of Religion* 30 (1991): 407-408.

Vernon, Glenn M. "The Religious 'Nones': A Neglected Category." *Journal for the Scientific Study of Religion* 7 (1968): 219-29.

Welch, Michael R. "The Unchurched: Black Religious Non-Affiliates." *Journal for the Scientific Study of Religion* 17 (1978): 290.

Wirth, Lewis. "Urbanism as a Way of Life." *American Journal of Sociology* 44 (1938): 3-24.

Wuthnow, Robert. "Recent Patterns of Secularization: A Problem of Generations?" *American Sociological Review* 41 (1976): 850-67.

_____, and Glen Mellinger. "Religious Loyalty, Defection, and Experimentation: A Longitudinal Analysis of University Men." *Review of Religious Research* 19 (1978): 234-45.

## Unpublished Works

Bongiovanni, Fred Wayne. "The Relationship Between Secularization and Transcendence Among Selected Contemporary Sociologists of Religion." Ph.D. dissertation, Southern Baptist Theological Seminary, 1984.

Marler, Penny Long. "A Dialectical Model for Understanding Secularization and American Religion, 1880–1935." Ph.D. dissertation, Southern Baptist Theological Seminary, 1991.

Waites, James. "A Future for Theological Education." Speech at Southern Baptist Theological Seminary, Louisville KY, recorded 2 September 1992.